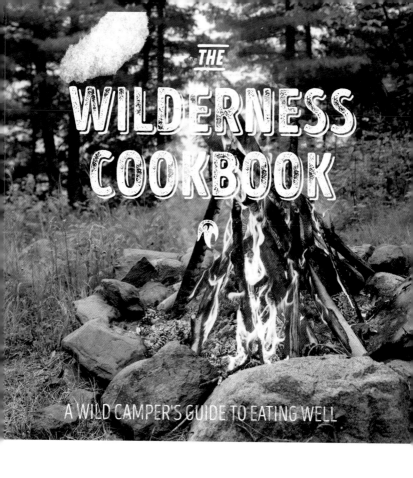

# THE WILDERNESS COOKBOOK

## A WILD CAMPER'S GUIDE TO EATING WELL

## PHOEBE SMITH

D1323705

Bradt

First published November 2018
Bradt Travel Guides Ltd
IDC House, The Vale, Chalfont St Peter, Bucks SL9 9RZ, England
www.bradtguides.com
Print edition published in the USA by The Globe Pequot Press Inc,
PO Box 480, Guilford, Connecticut 06437-0480

Text copyright © 2018 Phoebe Smith
Maps copyright © 2018 Bradt Travel Guides Ltd
Photographs copyright © 2018 Individual photographers (see below)
Project Managers: Anna Moores and Claire Strange
Cover design and research: Pepi Bluck, Perfect Picture
Design: Pepi Bluck, Perfect Picture

ISBN: 978 1 78477 076 1

**British Library Cataloguing in Publication Data**
A catalogue record for this book is available from the British Library

**Photographs**
All photographs © 2018 Liz Seabrook, except for individual photographers credited beside images and also those from picture libraries/tourist boards, credited as follows: Alamy Stock Photos (A), Shutterstock. com (S), SuperStock (SS), Visit Scotland (VS)
*Front cover* Wild camping on the shores of Loch Ericht, Scotland (Phoebe Smith); Rosemary and garlic mushrooms
*Back cover* Preparing breakfast in the dew
*Title page* Fire! (SS)
*Author photo on page 3* (William Parsons)
*Recipe shoot location* Little Walnut Hut, Walnuts Farm, Old Heathfield, East Sussex (booked via Sawdays Canopy & Stars; canopyandstars.co.uk)

**Maps**
David McCutcheon FBCart.S

Typeset by Pepi Bluck, Perfect Picture
Production managed by Jellyfish Print Solutions; printed in India
Digital conversion by www.dataworks.co.in

# ABOUT THE AUTHOR

By day Phoebe Smith is an award-winning travel writer, broadcaster and presenter as well as Editor-at-Large of *Wanderlust* travel magazine and Sleep Storyteller-in-Residence at  calm.com where she writes scripts for the likes of Stephen Fry, Joanne Lumley and Danai Gurira. By night she's an extreme-sleeping outdoors adventurer who thrives on heading to the wildest locations she can find in order to sleep in the strangest places she can seek out.

Phoebe was the first person to sleep at all the extreme points of mainland Britain – including the centremost location – which she did solo, on consecutive nights in 2014. In December 2017 she gave up her Christmas to complete the self-devised Sleep the Three Peaks challenge – in which she overnighted on the summits of the highest mountains in Wales, England and Scotland – raising both £8,000 and awareness for Centrepoint (the young people's homeless charity).

Phoebe is the author of eight books including the bestselling *Extreme Sleeps: Adventures of a Wild Camper*, *Wilderness Weekends: Wild Adventures in Britain's Rugged Corners* and the first guidebook to Britain's free-to-stay mountain shelters – *Book of the Bothy*.

Phoebe has proudly been an Ordnance Survey #GetOutside Champion since 2016 in recognition of her work encouraging people to enjoy the great outdoors. She is ambassador for the annual Big Canopy Campout (which helps raise funds for the

World Land Trust), as well as Wild Night Out, the UK's national night of adventure. She is also President of the Long Distance Walkers Association. Phoebe's ongoing mission is to prove that Britain offers adventure to rival anything you'll find overseas and that you don't need to be a beard-sporting, rufty-tufty, I'll-eat-a-dead-sheep-carcass Bear Grylls-type to have an adventure!

# ACKNOWLEDGEMENTS

There are so many people who have helped me while writing this book – from friends who have made me laugh to those who have offered much-needed guidance and counsel. So, in no particular order, I'd like to thank the following: Caz for making me sit down and actually write up the recipes; Liz for the wonderful photos; Kev for doing more washing-up than he ever signed up for; Doreen, Caro and Mark for endless support (Doreen we all miss you every day); Daniel and John for the beer and putting up with my WhatsApp rants; Sue for listening (don't worry – your copy's coming …); Danny for the invariably wise advice; my old editorial team at Wanderlust (aka 'the boys') comprising Tom, Rhodders, Gareth, Mike and Des (I couldn't have asked for a better crew; thank you for everything); Ollie and John for a welcome distraction; Fritha and Michael at Walnut Farm and Katie at Canopy & Stars for providing such a perfect place for us to photograph my culinary creations; Brian for taking on my admin (when I let him); and to the entire Bradt team for publishing this third book in my British wilderness series. And last, but by no means least, to my dad who has been my rock and the source of light whenever I've found it got too dark.

# CONTENTS

# INTRODUCTION

*'One cannot think well, love well, sleep well,
if one has not dined well.'*

Virginia Woolf

'All food tastes great outside' was a sentiment to which I had always ascribed. Having been a wilderness addict for the last 12 years, hell-bent on finding and sleeping in remote locations, my favourite moment – after hours toiling through all kinds of testing terrain – has always been when I finally come to a stop, set up my camp and prepare a hot meal as reward for my efforts.

The astute among you will have noticed the use of the word 'was', rather than 'is', in my first sentence. This is critical. Allow me to explain. Up until about five years ago I believed it completely. Food always did taste good when eaten outdoors. When consumed atop a mountain, deep in the forest or high on moorland in the porch of a tent while being pushed and pulled by the wind, curries, cup-a-soups – and even the dreaded Pot Noodles – genuinely did take on a superior flavour than when eaten at home.

Then, one day it happened. The trip started out like many before it. I meticulously checked that I had enough food to last me for a three-night escapade in Scotland – from breakfast to dinner plus an array of snacks. I headed out in the rain (it's OK, I'm used to it – and in my experience food often tastes better in the rain too) and after an 9-hour trudge that involved dodging bogs, ascending paths that resembled streams and battling hail driving into the face, I finally found a loch next to which I could pitch my tent.

I was utterly exhausted. Anything would taste good … or so I thought. I boiled water on my camping stove, poured it on to my dehydrated meal, stirred well and waited the required 8 minutes.

During that time my hunger burgeoned. I became ravenous, my mouth watering at the mere thought of warm food in my belly. Salivating, I gave the meal one last stir then dug in. It was horrible. Not just mildly unpleasant, not just somewhat tasteless – but the sort of utterly-overpowered-by-too-much-bad-flavour-piece-of-chewy-something-or-other that forced me to gag. I added a little more water, waited some more and stirred again. But each mouthful was as awful as the previous. Being hungry and having rationed supplies forced me to continue to eat. I managed about half before admitting defeat. I went to bed cold and hungry, swearing that I would never again use that particular brand of camping meal.

I hoped that my experience would be down to a one-off rogue bad flavour: these things do happen. But the next day, a similar problem occurred. At the end of my mini-expedition I was so hungry and tired that I couldn't even enjoy the glorious surrounds – the whole reason for my visit.

I chalked the above down to bad luck and thought no more about it – although I did become cautious about relying on any single brand of outdoor meal. After that I occasionally had a 'pouch-prepped' dish that didn't quite hit the spot, but assumed that I must be getting fussy. Until 2017, when the culinary nightmare returned – this time, with a vengeance.

I was near the end of a much more committing trip, walking alone along Greenland's Arctic Circle Trail. This was an ice-cap-to-ocean eight-dayer that demanded I carry all food necessary in my rucksack. I prepared sensibly, planning each meal carefully, opting for maximum calories with minimum weight, and throwing in calorific and tried-and-tested treats.

I did well. Most meals were good, and my bag got lighter by the day. Then, on the final evening, something remarkable happened. The weather was dreadful: gales and intense rain, wet-to-your-underwear, wish-I-was-anywhere-but-here appalling. But I happened upon a small hikers' hut that offered views down the yawning fjord and the imminent ocean. Amazingly, a previous visitor had kindly (or so I thought, at the time) left a pre-packed breakfast meal of muesli with orange. For the avoidance of doubt, a note was attached that invited a weary walker (me! Definitely me!) to enjoy.

I had never felt so ecstatic. With this beauty to look forward to in the morning, I abandoned caution and gorged myself on nearly all my remaining food. It meant my bag would be lighter. And I would go to bed content and full, with a wonderfully energy-packed brekkie ready for my waking. Winner, I thought.

Dawn arrived and so too breakfast. A meal I will never forget, for all the wrong reasons – the worst morning spread of my life. I followed the instructions and began eating. Bearing in mind that I was beyond hungry, you would have thought that the muesli would barely touch the sides.

But the opposite was true. It was repulsive – worse than that – it was frankly inedible. To be clear, nothing was ostensibly wrong with the meal: it was in date, completely sealed and prepared properly. Yet after three spoonfuls I gave up and silently (or possibly very, very loudly) cursed the evil hiker who had gifted me this work of the devil.

That day – my last day on the trail – was hard. With no good breakfast to sustain me, I struggled. The weather got worse, my tummy kept rumbling, and I felt ill for most of what should have been a triumphant finale. Finally arriving in Greenland's second-largest (but still tiny) city of Sisimiut, I was prepared to spend silly money to get lashings of food and coffee. It was at that moment that I made a promise to myself to start to explore homemade recipes that I could make in the wilds rather than relying on pre-packaged 'food'.

That pledge led to the birth of this book. It isn't about health kicks. It isn't about travelling with an entire kitchen set-up to make tasty grub (in contrast to many camping cookbooks, which assume we are happy to cart around a cast-iron Dutch oven). It is just about good food in wild places – nourishment so that you can get on with enjoying being outside.

But this book is about more than just food. To me, location is just as an important ingredient as the meal itself (see *Introducing the 'secret ingredient' …*, page 34). Accordingly, I have not only structured the book across five different landscapes but also sprinkled through its pages suggestions of where best to enjoy your culinary creations.

Whether you sleep a single night on a small hill or big mountain, opt for breakfast in your local wood, cross a moorland with your bivvy, paddle down a river or stride along the coast, I hope that this book helps you to truly, once-and-for-all realise – as I did – that *good* food tastes even better outside.

*Happy camping – and cooking …*

**Phoebe Smith, 2018**

· WELCOME ·

TO

# WILDERNESS COOKING

**P**ick up a camper's or backpacker's cookbook and they all seem to make the same three assumptions. First, you have a backpack large enough to transport the entire contents of your Tesco Extra shop, double-hob oven, huge cast-iron pans and skillets. Second, you have a back strong enough to carry said contents. Third, your car will be nearby so you can nip out at the drop of a hat for extras that you've forgotten.

At the other end of the scale you have the foraging books. Don't get me wrong, I love these and wish I had the confidence to live off the land. But they seem to assume that you wish to be a Ray Mears/Bear Grylls hybrid who doesn't bat an eyelid at the thought of drinking your own urine, while stumbling across wild food at every turn of the trail. That's all well and good. But what about us mere mortals who are petrified of picking the wrong thing or who have forgotten that summer is not the season for fungi, cockles or sheep carcasses (granted, perhaps the last are around in the warmer months – but why would you ever do that?).

And so to this book. I've approached it from the perspective of a wild camper who tends to follow a fairly last-minute whim to head outdoors. I've thus made the following three assumptions:

1. You need to carry everything you need – including camping gear – in a rucksack of 50–60 litres;
2. The only place to buy something en route will likely be an all-night garage, local store or small supermarket; and
3. You only have a single hob on which to cook.

To make things easier, feel free to mix some ingredients in advance, whether at home or in the car/accommodation/train before you hit the trail. Popping the contents in reusable containers avoids carrying unneeded extras such as excess packaging and reduces the amount of rubbish you will need to carry out with you.

# PREPARING
## FOR
# SUCCESS

As a wild camper who wants to cook their own meals rather than relying on pre-packed food, I suggest that you keep to hand – whether in what I call your 'Go Bag' (see opposite) or in your car boot – a set of containers plus frequently used, non-perishable ingredients that you can raid whenever needed.

PHOEBE SMITH

↑ Preparing a 'Go-Bag' in advance of your trip can help you take off when the mood takes you – with minimum delays

## WHAT TO PUT IN YOUR GO BAG

TOP
TIP

One tip I always offer those who want to explore the outdoors is to have what I call a 'Go Bag' ready packed at all times. It's basically a rucksack I keep, either next to my front door or in the boot of my car, filled with all the essentials I need for at least one night's wild camping – including food. That way, if the mood takes me or the opportunity or weather window arises, I have no excuses. I'm ready for my wild weekend.

Choose a bag with a capacity of around 50 litres. I use a women-specific pack but you should try on as many as possible – full – to find what sits best on your body shape. It should contain the following:

- Tent/bivvy
- Sleeping mat
- Sleeping bag
- Camping stove and pot/ pan(preferably with measurement markers on the side)
- Knife
- Small spatula
- Plate
- Chopping board
- Collapsible water container
- Matches
- Lighter
- Firesteel
- Gas
- Spork (spoon/knife/fork combination)
- Mug
- First-aid kit

- Head torch
- 'Bedtime dry bag' including: inflatable pillow, toothbrush and paste, dry socks, change of underwear, tissues, thermal base layer trousers
- 'Accessories dry bag', including warm gloves, hat and buff
- Fleece/midlayer top
- Waterproof jacket
- Insulated jacket
- Waterproof overtrousers
- Water bottle
- Food
- More food
- Walking poles
- Insect repellent
- Sunscreen
- Hand sanitiser

# IN THE CAMPER'S LARDER

To be ready to make some of these sumptuous dishes, I recommend that you keep in your arsenal the following if they are consistent with your dietary preferences:

## SPICES & HERBS

- Paprika
- Chilli powder
- Ground cinnamon
- Ground coriander
- Ground cumin
- Dried basil
- Dried mint
- All-season spice
- Turmeric
- Salt
- Black pepper

## CONDIMENTS

- Granulated sugar
- Demerara/brown sugar
- Soy/Worcestershire sauce
- Tabasco sauce

## FLAVOUR MAKERS

- Curry paste
- Jif squeezy lemon juice
- Soya-based 'bacon bits'

## BAKING STAPLES

- Milk powder
- Cooking oil (transferred into a small, refillable spray bottle for easy carrying – see 'Transporting & Storing Food / Supplies', see opposite)
- Baking powder
- Plain flour
- Marshmallows
- Free-range medium eggs

## USEFUL EXTRAS (PERISHABLE - BUT LONG-LIFE):

- 1 bag sponge cake mix
- 1 pre-packed scone mix
- 1 pre-packed pizza base mix
- Boil-in-the-bag rice sachets
- Peanut butter

WORTH KEEPING IN THE FRIDGE AT HOME TO GRAB ON YOUR WAY OUT:

- Sticks of butter
- Pre-grated cheese

## NO SUCH THING AS A FREE MEAL ...?

While there may not be free meals up for grabs, service stations, hotels and fast-food restaurants that may be on your way to your chosen camp spot tend to offer an array of handy pocket-size freebies for customers. So while you're munching your burger, perhaps you can take an extra sachet or two for future use.

- Small jar honey (can always refill at home)
- Small jam sachet/jar
- Butter sachets
- Milk sachets (long-life)
- Salt packets
- Sugar sachets
- Pepper packets
- Ketchup sachets
- Mustard sachets
- Mayonnaise sachets

## TRANSPORTING & STORING FOOD/SUPPLIES

Once you have your ingredients – whether kept separate or mixed at home – you will need to carry them in to your chosen camp spot. Obviously, weight is an issue – which is why you would never want to lug around canned goods – so empty them into something that keeps them fresh before hiking.

Reusable plastic containers with lids – as opposed to expensive and environmentally harmful single-use plastic bags – are cheap and last well. I recommend Light My Fire ( lightmyfire.com), a Scandinavian brand that not only manufactures a brilliant spork (spoon, knife and fork in a single utensil), but also produces a fantastic range of Tupperware-type items designed for the outdoors.

Best is the MealKit 2.0, which comes with a plate, bowl, two food boxes, collapsible cup with liquid-measuring lines – key for many

## KEEPING THINGS FRESH

Keeping perishables – such as milk, eggs, fish, meat and Quorn – fresh is important. Using airtight containers and reusable bags helps, but there are other ways too. Cold rivers and lakes can be an easy way to keep things cool (and fresh) so that they don't spoil. Just make sure that they don't drift away: use dry bags attached to branches, say, or wedge between rocks! Be mindful where you stop, so that you keep perishables in the shade. Use a light-coloured dry bag, which won't absorb heat.

In properly wintry conditions, simply leave sealed bags outside in the snow and they will be nice and cool by morning. If it's so cold that produce might freeze, however, consider keeping them close to you inside the tent. On multi-day trips, prioritise eating food that goes off quicker, such as meat or fresh Quorn.

of these recipes so you can get the consistencies right without having to guess, a combined strainer/cutting board and a spork – which all packs inside itself. I also like the Salt and Pepper Plus, which stores up to three spices.

For things like premixed stew etc, then opt for reusable storage bags. Stasher (⊘ stasher.com) do a great yet inexpensive one that is made from silicone so is completely plastic-free – making it better for the environment. You can use them to boil food, and they are freezer- and dishwasher-safe.

## REMEMBER THE LITTLE THINGS ...

Once you've bought the items you need, I suggest doing the following, which will make your life a little easier:

- Empty can contents into reusable bags.
- Invest in reusable egg caddies/carriers to avoid messy breakages.
- Don't take a whole block of butter – cut off only the quantity you'll need.

- Buy pre-grated cheese (or grate your own pre-trip).
- If buying supplies in jars (eg: peanut butter, pesto, honey), scoop some into a reusable container and leave the rest in the car or at home.
- Empty cooking oil into a small, reusable bottle (with spray top if possible).
- Keep a small selection of required spices in a reusable, compartmentalised container or in little envelopes of foil.
- Transfer alcohol into a hipflask or similar.
- Before you set out, weigh different amounts of flour etc so that you become familiar with what they look like. Knowing that 400g of flour is about half the capacity of your mess tin or a full camping mug will mean that you can manage without weighing scales.

## ESSENTIAL UTENSILS

You don't need masses of equipment for camp cooking, but it helps to take the basics. So …

### FOR THE BACKPACK

- A good, sharp knife
- 1 spork
- Mug (use for soup, porridge or granola as well as drinks)
- Bowl/plate (choose models with collapsible sides that serve as both items of 'crockery')
- Water bottle (for your drinking water)
- Water container (go for a collapsible or foldaway model with a wide mouth: this is for collecting water for cooking or washing-up)
- Rubbish bag (see *Responsible camping and cooking*, page 22)
- Camping stove (see *Camping stoves*, page 18)
- Pot/mess tin
- Frying pan (depending on your recipe)
- Measuring cup (good camping pots and stoves come with measurements marked)

### FOR THE CAR

- Can opener
- Small, reusable jars
- Tupperware/bags
- Bottle opener
- Foil
- Silicone paper

## EXTRAS THAT CAN MAKE THINGS EASIER (THOUGH NOT ESSENTIAL)

- Firesteel (a rod made of friction-ignited burning metal that produces sparks when struck with the accompanying striker) will always work even when a lighter and matches won't.
- Spatula (Jetboil ✐ jetboil.com produces a good, collapsible, lightweight one).
- Cooking 'fork' (sold by Light My Fire ✐ lightmyfire.com, the GrandPa's FireFork attaches to the end of any stick) and is great for toasting marshmallows.

# COOKING METHODS

## CAMPING STOVES

An abundance of brands of camping stove vies for your hard-earned cash. So it's worth understanding the types of cooking apparatus available, together with their pros and cons to help you choose between the different fuels. All will need lighting, so always take more than one lighting method with you, in case your preferred option fails.

PHOEBE SMITH

### Gas

Whether a complete cooking system (with inbuilt pots etc) or a simple foldaway mini-stove, these bad boys tend to screw on to pressurised-gas cylinders that are available in multiple sizes from most outdoor shops, some supermarkets and even local stores in rural areas. Always opt for screw-in models, which are safer and easier to use than those you have to pierce. My recommended models are Jetboil and Primus.

**Pros:** fast, easy-to-control flame (so you can simmer etc), very efficient and lightweight.

**Cons:** can be difficult to gauge how much gas you have left (meaning you may have to carry extra on longer trips), sometimes temperamental in cold weather.

### Liquid fuel

The Duke of Edinburgh (DofE) award-approved Trangia is the poster child for this type of stove. They usually use methylated spirits (meths), paraffin, kerosene or even petrol (just don't mix them!). Store the liquid in a sturdy fuel bottle, then pour in to the burner and light.

**Pros:** ignites easily, works well even in the cold, fuel is easy to source pre-trip.

**Cons:** doesn't burn as hot as other fuels (especially gas) so can take longer to boil water, so you may need to carry more fuel.

### Fuel tablet

Anyone who has ever seen a military survival kit will be familiar with this type of fuel. In short, it comprises a hexamine tablet burnt inside a little metal 'stove'. Pick one up cheaply from army-surplus stores.

**Pros:** light, simple to use, long shelf life.

**Cons:** flame cannot be controlled so really only good for boiling water; can be temperamental in cold or wind; burning can produce a toxic mix of chemicals so food must be cooked in containers with lids; can leave a sticky residue on pots.

## Foraged fuel

Often the most fun – at least in theory. For me, this is the best option if you want to experience the joy of a campfire, but aren't allowed to light one or are worried about scorching the land. The ideal model is the Irish-made Kelly Kettle ($\mathcal{O}$ kellykettle.com), which is available in a number of sizes. You can burn pretty much anything natural in the base – from wood to dry animal dung. Then boil water in the chimney or cook your food using the grill/pot rest on top.

**Pros:** fun to source fuel, perfect for toasting marshmallows.

**Cons:** if you can't find fuel or light a fire you will go hungry; you have to constantly worry about finding more fuel; flame cannot be controlled; the heaviest option.

## FIRE!

If you intend to build a fire (page 190) on which to cook, toast marshmallows, or provide the centrepiece of campside merriment, do ensure you have permission from a landowner or confirm that fires are allowed. Coastal areas and riversides are definitely best for cooking over a fire. You can build it in the sand/rocks without risking it spreading; there's water nearby just in case and it leaves no trace. In moorland, mountains and forests, you risk destroying ecosystems so an open fire is to be avoided.

A Kelly Kettle (see above) is a responsible alternative to an open fire. Of course, if you're in the mountains or other wild place you may be near to a bothy, which usually has its own stove/fireplace. If you do have a fire be sure to extinguish it before you leave and to clear the area of debris. A responsible camp cook (page 22) never leaves any trace.

As with camping stoves, always take more than one lighting method in case your matches/lighter fails you.

## ADDED EXTRAS

Although making your own food is clearly the purpose of this book, don't forget that you should always take some quick-and-easy instant wins when camping too. These enable you to concentrate on your cooking without being distracted by hunger pangs. What you carry depends on personal choice, but the aim is to give you an instant energy hit. Personally, I always take with me: sachets of hot chocolate, coffee (two-in-one sachets, as I take milk), Belvita biscuit packets (⏀ belvitabreakfast.com), chocolate bars, cereal bars, peanuts and dried fruit. Keep a lookout throughout the forthcoming chapters for 'Camper's hacks' — handy hints and tips to make your camping life easier.

# RESPONSIBLE CAMPING *AND* COOKING

You don't want your actions to ruin the experience for future campers. So act responsibly by following these handy guidelines:

- Pack out everything that you take in, including used foil and food packaging.
- Be mindful of where you wash up: bury any food waste rather than chucking it on the ground or in rivers.
- Use environmentally friendly washing-up liquid – that is non-toxic, biodegradable, and free from harsh chemicals (such as Dr Bronner's Sal Suds Biodegradable Cleaner or Puracy's Dish Soap).

## FINDING & CREATING THE PERFECT CAMPING KITCHEN

My expectation, given that you are reading this book, is that you are planning on 'going wild' with your cooking, rather than 'cheating' in a campsite offering such luxuries as sinks, running water and rubbish bins merely feet away! Assuming that to be the case, here are some features to think about when looking for the perfect camp/cook spot:

- **Ground:** look for level ground on which to position your camping stove. Ideally, place it a little distance away from your tent, just to be safe. Never ever cook inside your tent!
- **Outlook:** a good view is mandatory!
- **Wind:** if the weather is bad then look for natural wind blocks to shelter your stove. In some terrain, your tent and/or body may be best placed for this job.
- **Water:** if there is a water source available, then it's handy to park yourself within a reasonable distance. Doing so means you can quickly source water for cooking and

cleaning. But don't go too close, particularly to still waterbodies, as water can be a breeding ground for midges.

- **Set up your waste collection first:** there's little more annoying than getting stuck in to your cooking then having nowhere to put the handful of rubbish you generate. So get a rubbish bag ready before you even start chopping that aubergine. In woodland, hang it from a tree; in open landscapes, use a convenient bush or hold it down with a rock to stop it blowing away.
- **Set up a 'prep' station:** lay out your raw ingredients on an empty dry bag or a plate. Read through the recipe before starting. Check all your required utensils are close to hand. Then chop all that needs chopping and slice all that needs slicing, and grease all that needs greasing (as these will be hard to do once cooking proper is underway).
- **Get cooking!**
- **After you've eaten . . . :** don't be lazy and simply crawl into your sleeping bag – no matter how tempting it is to 'wait until the morning'. First, pack away excess food, clean the pots and bag your rubbish.

Taking a handful of fresh mint leaves can make multiple cups of tea to sup while prepping your meal ↑

# WILD-CAMPING ETIQUETTE

If you are cooking in the wild, then you are assuredly camping in the wild too. Here are a few things to think about – from accommodation to when you need to 'go' …

### TOILET TALK

Without trying to sugar-coat the issue at all, what goes in, must … ahem … come out. Accordingly, when wild camping it is important that you set up a toilet responsibly. To do that, do the following:

- Find a spot away from your kitchen (naturally) and at least 30m (around 30 strides) away from any water source, path or bothy.
- Using a stick or stone, dig a hole in the ground around 15cm deep. It might be useful to mark it with a rock or branch so you can find it again later.
- If it didn't come out of you, don't put it in the hole. This means all toilet paper needs to be packed out with your rubbish to avoid it being dug up by animals.
- When you've finished, fill in the hole so that you leave no trace of your visit.

# PURIFYING WATER

You need water for most recipes and you will certainly need to drink it. Some landscapes lack abundant water sources so you may have to carry water in your supplies. If there is water, it's always good practice to purify it. Look for fast-flowing streams or rivers – or at least water where there is some movement. Avoid stagnant pools. It's best to collect water well away from any bothies or huts and you should be particularly careful if close to farmland as you have no idea what people or animals have done in the water.

Once you have got hold of your water, check whether it needs filtering. If you've followed the above advice, barring a few bits of grass (which you can pick out with your hands), it should be fine. If it needs filtering, an emergency option is to pour it through a clean sock. Once you've done that, what are the options for making the water safe to drink?

- **Boiling:** the tried, tested and highly recommended way to treat any water – and seeing as you already have a stove with you to cook with, no extra kit is required. It usually takes several minutes to get it bubbling. Once there, let it do a 'rolling boil' (fast simmer) for a further 2 minutes). This method will kill any nasties.
- **Chlorine drops/treatment tablets:** these are effective at killing viruses and bacteria, though do tend to leave an unpleasant aftertaste. You will also need to carry enough tablets to cover all your water needs.
- **UV light treatment:** this is great for destroying bacteria, viruses and parasites in just a couple of minutes. However, the process can be time-consuming and works only with precise quantities of water. Moreover, the equipment is a little fragile and you'll need to take enough batteries with you to power it for all your needs.
- **Microfilters:** these squeeze water through microscopic holes, trapping the nasties within. They are very good at removing bacteria and parasites. Some brands also remove viruses but others need to be used in tandem with chlorine drops. The only issues are the extra weight and bulk compared with other purification devices, the extra effort required to make them work (they are normally pump action) and the fact that filters need replacing after treating a set number of litres of water.

NEIL S PRICE

Consider taking a collapsible and reusable water container ↑
when wild camping – it will take up less space in your pack

# WHAT KIND OF CAMPER ARE YOU?

*Bivvy, bothy, tent, tarp or hammock?*
*When it comes to camping you've a whole array of accommodation*
*options, so how do you know which is right for you?*
*Try answering this series of questions to decide …*

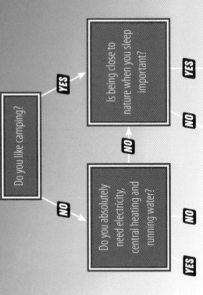

Do you like camping?

**NO** → Do you absolutely need electricity, central heating and running water?

**YES** → Is being close to nature when you sleep important?

Do you absolutely need electricity, central heating and running water? **NO** → Is being close to nature when you sleep important?

Is being close to nature when you sleep important?
**NO**    **YES**

Do you absolutely need electricity, central heating and running water?
**NO**    **YES**

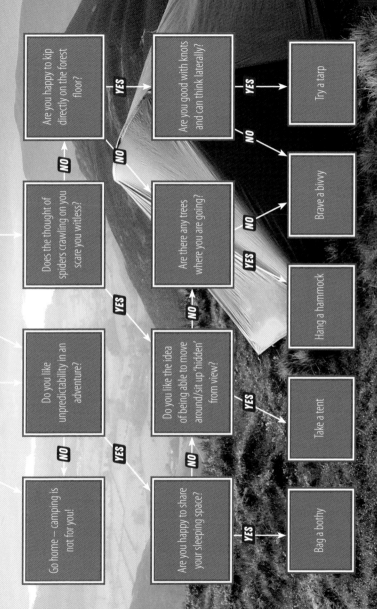

Go home – camping is not for you!

Do you like unpredictability in an adventure?

**NO** → Go home – camping is not for you!

Does the thought of spiders crawling on you scare you witless?

**NO** → Are you happy to kip directly on the forest floor?

Are you happy to kip directly on the forest floor?
**YES** → Are you good with knots and can think laterally?
**NO** → Are there any trees where you are going?

Are you good with knots and can think laterally?
**YES** → Try a tarp
**NO** → Brave a bivvy

Are there any trees where you are going?
**NO** → Brave a bivvy
**YES** → Hang a hammock

Do you like the idea of being able to move around/sit up 'hidden' from view?
**NO** → Are there any trees where you are going?
**YES** → Take a tent

Are you happy to share your sleeping space?
**NO** → Do you like the idea of being able to move around/sit up 'hidden' from view?
**YES** → Bag a bothy

(STEWART SMITH/A)

# USING *THIS* GUIDE

## CAMPER'S HACKS

Within some recipes you will notice that I have peppered in what I call 'camper's hacks'. These are simply little tips to make your life easier – from buying something pre-packed to using a substitute item. You're welcome!

### FORAGE OR NOT TO FORAGE?

You'll note that each chapter suggests plants and fungi that may be available to collect for free in that particular landscape. As this book is not intended to be a foraging guide, I've stuck purposefully to abundant and easy-to-recognise species. I also provide specific instructions about the use of each.

The golden rule with foraging is 'if in doubt, spit it out'! Or, alternatively, 'if not sure, buy from the store'! Competent and confident foraging takes considerable practice and expertise (whether your knowledge has been gained from a dedicated book or a course led by an expert). Let's be honest, you can literally worry yourself sick if you're not sure whether something is safe to eat. Even wild-food guru Ray Mears says that he constantly learns about new species to eat, so foraging is a skill that takes a lifetime to master.

### THE ART OF IMPROV

By far the most important skill for a camping chef to learn is how to substitute one item – or utensil – for another. Things break or go wrong. You forget something or your stove won't light. So you need to think on your feet. Here are a few handy suggestions or items to keep in mind (or car or rucksack) …

# MUSHROOM SAFETY

Be especially aware of mushrooms and other fungi which can be very hard to identify as some edible species are visually similar to poisonous varieties. The consequences of making a mistake can be lethal. Don't take the risk unless you are 100% certain that what you are eating is safe.

Think and look very carefully before even handling fungi – some can cause irritation to your skin (NEIL S PRICE)

- Duct tape can fix just about anything. Wrap a strip around your walking pole or rucksack strap to keep it sticky for if you need it.
- Covering some dishes with a 'lid' will help them cook evenly. Should you lose, forget or not have a lid, think laterally. Use your plate/a flat rock/large leaf . . .
- See the elements as your friend, not enemy. Snow serves as your freezer. A stream becomes your fridge. Blazing sunshine (we can dream!) keeps food warm.
- Take a backup: there will come a time when your camping stove does not work. The key thing is not to panic. The most likely explanation is that the stove has got wet – often from placing a water-filled pot on top of it. Dry the stove thoroughly and try again. Inbuilt igniters can break too so always take a backup. Firesteel is best as it works even if wet; otherwise waterproof matches are good.
- Be ready to eat what you can without a stove: if it all goes wrong such that the stove breaks, the fire won't start and you're hungry, look at your ingredients carefully. There will always be something you can eat cold. It might not be the best meal, but at least it is a meal. Moreover, you will be sure to not let what went wrong happen again (or so you'll tell yourself . . .).

# IN THE BAG . . .

If, after reading this book, you think heading into the wilderness sounds delightful, but you're feeling a bit lazy and prefer to opt for a ready-made meal … don't worry, I'm not judging you (much). But do bear in mind the following:

## THE OPTIONS

There are two types of camping meal: dehydrated and pre-cooked. The former has the advantage of being lightweight, with a great calorie-to-gram ratio and only requires you to boil water (and patiently wait up to 10 minutes) before eating. However, some taste better than others, and they are usually packed to the brim with chemicals, salt and fat. Pre-cooked meals are often a little nicer than dehydrated ones, with fewer chemicals. To save on washing-up, I always opt for meals that you can boil in the bag. Some, however, need to be cooked in a pot, so be warned and read instructions carefully. Pre-cooked meals contain water so are obviously heavier than dehydrated versions. But they have one distinct advantage: if your stove breaks you can still eat the contents (albeit cold).

## CHOICES

Among the abundance of choice available at good camping stores, here are a few brands I recommend:

### Dehydrated

* **Tent Meals (⌕ tentmeals.co.uk):** produces meals that you need to cook in your stove pot (rather than boil in the bag). However, the breakfasts and Moroccan meals are worth the effort – and they all come with a lovely handwritten note . . .
* **Firepot (⌕ outdoorfood.com):** handmade in Dorset with only natural ingredients and no chemicals. The only downside is the small range, although all of it is good!
* **Adventure Food (⌕ adventurefood.com):** I particularly like the 'curry fruit rice' and vegetable hotpot.

PHOEBE SMITH

Pre-packed camping meals are a lazy option, but if you must, make sure you pick a tried-and-tested one ... ↑

### Ready-to-eat

- **Forestia (⊘ weareforestia.com):** great vegetarian options, particularly the (veggie) meatballs with pasta.
- **Beyond The Beaten Track (⊘ beyondthebeatentrack.com):** the vegetarian sausage and tomato breakfast is good at any time of the day!
- **Wayfarer (⊘ vango.co.uk):** the chocolate and sticky toffee pudding is by far the best of their selection.

## PIMP YOUR PACKET

Even if you resort to a pre-packed camping meal you can jazz it up a bit with a few little extras, such as:

- Spices (particularly good are paprika and cumin)
- Raisins (sweetens the blandest dishes)
- Sundried tomatoes (makes a cheap dish feel a bit more classy)
- Couscous (helps bulk up the meal and add some carbs – good with curry that comes without rice)
- Cheese (brings flavour and adds moisture to a dish)
- Bread (when doesn't a slice make things into more of a meal?!)

## SAFETY FIRST

Going into the wilderness and wild cooking both come with considerable but manageable risks. The author and publisher have done all they can to ensure the accuracy of recipes and suggested locations to enjoy the food. But they cannot be held legally or financially responsible for any accident, injury, loss or inconvenience (or bad-tasting dishes!) as a result of information or advice contained in this book. Any outdoor activity – including anything that involves fire or cooking stoves – is always undertaken entirely at your own risk. Finally, please: never EVER try to cook in your tent, no matter how cold it is.

STOCK-ASSO/S

# A NOTE ABOUT RECIPE SELECTION

You'll undoubtedly note that most recipes in this book do not contain meat or fish. The reason is two-fold. Firstly, I am a vegetarian – a proper one rather than a faux vegetarian (aka pescatarian) who confuses the non-veggie public into believing that we eat fish (we don't). Therefore I feel best qualified to recommend recipes that are meat-free. I hope you'll agree, finding them so tasty that you barely even notice the absence of animal.

The second reason is practicality: decent cuts of meat and fish are tricky to buy in all-night garages and service stations en route to the wilderness. The third reason is hygiene. Meat and fish are hard to keep fresh and the consequences of eating gone-off examples are much more dire than if, for instance, you were to eat a wilted carrot. This reason alone is why most meat-eaters I know happily forgo their prized staple when going wild.

I have tried and tested all recipes in this book over many years. They represent my very favourite outdoor meals. Some are my own version of well-known camping fare. Many may be meals that you may not have thought of making before. And some are just plain fun. I hope you enjoy making them as much as you do eating them …

PHOEBE SMITH

# INTRODUCING _THE_ 'SECRET INGREDIENT'...

When it comes to outdoor food, I truly believe that the location is a prime and often very much overlooked part of the recipe.

I recall one trip to Wales where I watched a family choosing to picnic in a car park. There's nothing wrong with that at all, and it probably suited young kids and older parents. But it wasn't a patch on my 'dining room' that evening – next to a lake, watching the sun descend behind a mountain. With this setting, I know that my meal tasted thousands of times better.

It is for this reason that this book is divided up, not by meals, but by landscapes. There are chapters covering coast and riverside, mountain and moorland plus, of course, our wonderful woodlands.

↑ Wild camping can command the best sunsets but lack of water sources must be a consideration

The recipes associated with each particular terrain are not chosen by accident. Instead they intentionally complement the surrounds, taking into consideration the resources available, whether this relates to foraging potential, the abundance (or lack of) water, the ease of building a responsible campfire, and the type of food you need to help you be at ease in that particular environment (eg: home comforts for climbing mountains, foods that build stamina for moors etc).

So to guarantee eating in your own personal five-star venue, do go and try the recipes here at any of the suggested spots. Then be inspired to find your own secret ingredient – a place special to you where you can delight in an exclusive dining experience ...

## FEEDBACK REQUEST

Been inspired to set up the camp stove in the wilderness? Or want to suggest a recipe that you feel should have been included? You can send your feedback direct to Bradt; contact us on ☎ 01753 893444 or ✉ info@bradtguides.com. We will forward emails to Phoebe who may post updates on the Bradt website at ☉ bradtupdates.com/wildernesscookbook. Alternatively, you can add a review of the book to ☉ bradtguides.com or Amazon.

Communicate your adventures on Twitter, Instagram, Facebook and YouTube using the hashtag #wildernesscookbook and we'll share it for you.

- ▮ Bradt Travel Guides & @ThePhoebeRSmith
- 🐦 @BradtGuides & @PhoebeRSmith
- 📷 @bradtguides & @PhoebeRSmith
- 📌 bradtguides
- ▶ You Tube www.youtube.com/user/extremesleeps

# MOORLAND

As seen here in the New Forest, heather is often a defining feature of moorland in Britain, as is mist.

There is no type of terrain quite like Britain's high moorland for creating an atmosphere that evokes the emotions and sharpens the senses. It's a place where there is often very little in the way of a distinct water source while, at the same time, water seems to be present all around you. You can often hear it when you stop: a faint babble or splutter, a barely audible trickle, or a pleasingly comforting saturated squelch beneath your boots. Then there is the trademark mist: haunting, moody and seemingly ever-present.

The British have been fascinated with moorland for centuries. Artists started it, painting the wide and wild expanses on long horizontal canvases, capturing people's imagination as they gazed into the tantalisingly barren scenes. Writers followed with Heathcliff and Cathy declaring their love for one another amid the tors and heather, before walking the moors together in an endless eternity in *Wuthering Heights*. And Sherlock Holmes took us with him as he journeyed deep within the bleakness of the high quivering quagmires, looking for the spectral canine in *The Hound of the Baskervilles*.

As much as 15% of the entire planet's moorland is in the British Isles so it's no wonder that this terrain defines the country more than any other. Moorland is characterised by its low-level vegetation due to mainly acidic soils, high altitudes and ample levels of rainfall, creating a mass of sopping wet ground that you can feel shake as you walk across it. More than 70% of moorland is covered with heather species, of which there are six in the British Isles.

*"There is no type of terrain quite like Britain's high moorland for creating an atmosphere"*

Despite the rain, there is something very special about moorland beyond the trademark mist and bogs. First, there's the diversity of flora and fauna. To the untrained eye, the land may look like a whole lot of mud and grass. But look a little closer and you'll realise that there's a plethora of moss species, furled coils of bracken, the purple shoots of (more than one species of) heather, and the white, feather-like wisps of cotton-grass. These different plant species support a diverse array of wildlife – some of which occur in very few places.

Some moors are home to long-legged mountain hares that scurry through the grass, foxes, red deer, field voles and even polecats and pine martens. Exmoor ponies live in the southwest of England, and Carneddau ponies in northwest Wales. The skies can fill with the swooping silhouettes of peregrine falcons and buzzards. Where wind-scoured tors crown rolling summits like castles, black ravens may squawk and goad, adding to the fairy-tale quality of the vista. Smaller species such as meadow pipit and wheatear dart out in front of your boot steps, startling you, and insects such as the decorative emperor moth and Scotch Argus butterfly hide amid the foliage before flitting upwards to salute the sun.

This landscape does, at first, appear completely wild – and feels it too. But another fascinating feature of British moorland that makes

## TICKS

On moorland where deer and sheep are present there is always a risk of Lyme disease-carrying ticks, particularly in long grass. Always check your body — especially creases on your legs, arms and groin — at the end of each day. Carry a tick-removal device with you. Never try to remove a tick that has latched on by burning or suffocating it, as this will cause it to regurgitate its stomach contents into your body, which increases the risk of transmitting the bacterial infection.

PHOEBE SMITH

it special is its connection to our ancestors. Scores of standing stones are found on moorlands, including the world's longest line, on Dartmoor. Remains of homesteads and mine workings from when industry was king also both demonstrate man's imprint on the moors which has been felt here for centuries.

You could also argue that moorland shows more evidence of prehistoric man's impact than any other type of landscape. This is because thousands of years ago it was covered in woodland. Many areas were deforested to make way for farming and grazing cattle and sheep, so today's environment is very different from the original vegetation cover. Even those areas that feel 'wild' – especially those stocked to the gills with grouse – are still very much 'managed' by humans to stay in a particular way – in fact grouse moors are now effectively heather monocultures, devoid of pretty much all other wildlife bar the red grouse purposefully bred and managed for shooting.

By far the most alluring aspect of moorland is the challenge it presents us. Often pockmarked with bogs of uncertain depths,

Dancing among one of the many stone circles on Dartmoor's high moorland – ↑
this one fittingly known as 'The Dancers' up on Erme Plains

**TOP TIP**

# HOW TO FIND SHELTER ON HIGH MOORLAND

Moorlands are often windy and wet places to be, so, when you stop for a snack you want to be sure you do it in as comfortable a spot as possible. First, look for natural shelter – tors, rocks or even slight depressions in the ground will make pitching a tent or stopping to cook much easier. Failing that, don't forget that your rucksack itself can make a good windbreak. Sit with it on and your back to the wind, using it to block gusts so you can cook without problems.

PHOEBE SMITH

↑ Tor very much – using Hound Tor's rocky outcrops in Dartmoor as natural wind breaks makes cooking a breeze

moorland can make walking even short distances tricky. Then there is the mist which can descend without warning; transforming a pleasant sunny day into a scary navigational challenge where the moorland's lack of topographical features makes orienting oneself on the basis of visual clues virtually impossible.

As if the physical demands of the moors weren't enough, it's the legends that are attached to them that will give us a psychological beating. They vary from tales of the Cu Saeng in Scotland – a ghost-like monster that patrols the high, barren plains and causes instant death to those who look at it – to rumours of escaped big cats. The latter could well be grounded in fact because the 1976 Dangerous Animals Act made it illegal to keep certain wild animals without a licence, which most people couldn't get. Since then, reports of the 'beasts of Dartmoor' have been frequent – and a local zoo even admitted that they freed three pumas during the 1980s.

Beasts (both real and imagined) aside, if you are tantalised by the moors it is imperative that you are able to navigate confidently and competently with map and compass in case any GPS device you carry malfunctions. Paths – even those shown on maps – are not always easy to find and are not always marked. Moreover, sheep tracks have a funny knack of resembling (human) rights of way.

You also need to be well equipped. Gear made for rain is absolutely vital and, as you don't want to risk lighting a fire and potentially damaging the sensitive ecosystem of the moors, you need to bring food you can cook on a stove rather than start a campfire. You'll also need energy-packed snacks to power you up and over the moorland's many undulations. Comfort food for the day's end is practically mandatory. Water can sometimes be tricky to find as you want a fast-flowing source rather than that found in the stagnant pools of a muddy bog. It pays to choose recipes that do not rely too heavily on a good local water supply – or alternatively you may decide to carry all you need with you.

# HOW TO GET YOURSELF OUT OF A BOG

The main risk with walking in the moors is the sudden and often unexpectedly soft ground underfoot. Falling into a bog is akin to stepping into quicksand so how you act should you do so is key to getting out safely.

1. Don't panic – advice not applicable solely to intergalactic space travel. When sinking into a cold and wet bog, you could easily be up to your chest in seconds, so it's easy to lose your cool. But don't. Waving arms and making frantic movements will actually see you sink quicker. So stop, and breathe.

2. If someone is with you, obviously alert them to the problem. Then calmly try to get yourself out of trouble. If you can remove your heavy rucksack do. Every movement should be slow and steady. Start by trying to lift a single leg out, initially moving it backwards so you don't fall on your face. It doesn't matter if this movement makes the other leg go deeper: getting one leg out first is good. Then try to move the other leg – always moving backwards.

3. If, however, you're already in it up to your waist, lie back and try to distribute your weight evenly. The aim is to essentially 'float' on the bog surface. Once you have done this, you can work on getting your legs out.

4. Once you have your legs out and are floating, roll yourself over again and again or wiggle your way across the bog on your back until you reach solid ground, then slowly and carefully pull yourself out. It is really important that you don't try to crawl or walk, otherwise it is likely that you will have to start the process all over again!

5. The key thing to remember is that bogs are avoidable and there are clues in the landscape that will help you identify trouble. For instance, during flowering season cotton grass (see photograph, above) is a key indicator of the location of waterlogged ground, as are the long green 'lashes' shown on OS maps, so keep your eyes peeled. It's also worth taking walking poles into moorland as you can always test the depth of a bog before attempting to step past it – and even vault yourself over particularly deep sections.

The beautiful but bog-laden High Moor of North York Moors National Park
(MIKE KIPLING PHOTOGRAPHY/A)

Potential hardships abound. Nevertheless, the idea of battling tough and unstable terrain and changeable weather seems to fire something up in many walkers' souls. Better yet, old byelaws mean that some patches of moorland allow wild camping. This means that spending the night outside, doing some wilderness cooking and even trying your hand at spotting both spirits and felines is a real possibility.

In short, moorland is beautifully British and ball-bustingly hard, but certainly worth the effort. If nothing else, the silence that pervades a misty plateau is reward enough for venturing there. Then throw in some particularly hearty and tasty grub that has never known a freeze-dried packet and you will undoubtedly (and sometimes inexplicably) find yourself desperate for more. More views, more food, more moors …

PAUL DANIELS/S

↑ The Peak District is perhaps one of the most notorious stretches of moorland in Britain

# SECRET INGREDIENTS

*So, you've found out about the attractions of moorlands, but which moorland will you go to? Here's a sprinkling of suitable spots to make each meal even more of a treat.*

## 1. DARTMOOR, DEVON, ENGLAND

What can be said of this wild, yawning beast of a moorland that hasn't already been described by some of our best-loved authors? Defined by its peak-adorning granite tors that have been shaped by the elements for millennia, it not only is the best moorland in which to let your imagination run wild with stories and legends, but also is the one place in England where you can legally wild camp. There are some exclusions due to military training, but on the whole you pretty much have free rein to take your tent – and, of course, your cooking pot – and go wild.

## 2. CARNEDDAU, SNOWDONIA, GWYNEDD, WALES

Often overlooked in favour of the more craggy landscape to its south, the Carneddau is a Welsh treasure peppered with relics and ruins from past human inhabitants. Check out the remains of the home of farmers who once lived high on this ground – now a bothy at Llyn Dulyn ('black lake'), which is the perfect place in which to prepare and even cook your meals. Then there are the

*"Here in this mix of*
*moor and mountain*
*the summits are secondary*
*to the sheer feeling of solitude"*

Dining in the wild high moors of Snowdonia's Carneddau will nourish your belly and your soul
(MATT GIBSON/S)

Welsh princes (and more recently princesses) who gave their names to the peaks. Here in this mix of moor and mountain, paths are not readily defined and the summits are secondary to the sheer feeling of solitude.

## 3. BLEAKLOW, PEAK DISTRICT, ENGLAND

Lying near the Derbyshire town of Glossop, this gritstone moor is famed for its quick-descending mist. Testament comes from the wreckage of a Superfortress bomber *Overexposed*, which fell victim to poor visibility one fateful day in 1948. All 13 members of a photographic squadron sadly lost their lives. Owing to the peat terrain, little of the wreckage could be safely removed, so it sits there still, a reminder of the power of nature and a place thick with an atmosphere so palpable you can almost feel it.

NEIL S PRICE

↑ Many parts of the World War II bomber in Bleaklow remain on the moorland, still very much intact

## 4. FOREST OF BOWLAND, LANCASHIRE, ENGLAND

Once a royal hunting ground that was home to wild boar, wildcat and even grey wolf, this windswept Lancashire stronghold formerly had a reputation among walkers for being hard to access. That was until the wonderful Countryside Rights of Way Act was passed in 2000, effectively opening up swathes of the out-of-bounds moorscape for hikers to explore. But very few do. And therein lies Bowland's appeal. Choose a section of moor and you're very likely to get it to yourself. A favourite place of mine is Whitendale Hanging Stones which marks the geographical centremost point of mainland Britain – an ideal spot at which to fire up the stove.

## 5. ELAN VALLEY, POWYS, WALES

With over 120km$^2$ of blanket bog, peat, heather, bog rosemary and mosses, you may be surprised to learn that this mid-Wales enclave isn't all about what's on the ground. In fact, you could argue that a visit here is very much about keeping one's eyes trained on the sky – both day and night. For the upland environment is the perfect nesting ground for golden plovers and dunlins – which you could encounter as they run about on the ground and the skies attract eight of the UK's rarest birds including the merlin. But even when the sun goes down and the stove comes out keep on glancing upwards. As an International Dark Sky Park, this is a world-class location for stargazing.

## 6. HOWGILLS, CUMBRIA, ENGLAND

Steadfastly in the shadow of its Lake District and Yorkshire Dales cousins, the high moorland fells of the Howgills are often ignored. Cleaved into subtle peaks and troughs by a series of deep gills, their upper ground is markedly boggy and often blanketed thickly in heather. Owing to the absence of other walkers this area feels even more isolated than other moorland, and the semi-wild and heavy-coated fell ponies that patrol the slopes add to the appealing end-of-the-world atmosphere. This place will have you hungry for more …

## 7. RANNOCH MOOR, GLENCOE, SCOTLAND

So tough is this trough of wet and wild moorland, that even the determined Victorians who built the train line had to resort to simply floating tracks across its expanse – utilising tree roots and natural debris to construct as stable a surface as possible. Surrounded by eye-watering, jaw-dropping mountains that seem to draw a secretive curtain around it, walking across the moor feels like you are truly far from civilisation – even if you did come by the Intercity service (there's a handy station at its centre). If camping here, when not keeping your eye out for the ankle-sucking (and oft-hidden) bogs, also keep a look out for the fabled Cu Saeng who is said to haunt the landscape looking for lost souls. With that in mind don't forget your map, and while you're there, you may as well pop the stove on, too …

"Walking across the moor
feels like you are truly far
from civilisation"

The haunting and remote-feeling Rannoch Moor
will heighten imaginations and require hearty food (SS)

# 8. NORTH YORK MOORS, NORTH YORKSHIRE, ENGLAND

It would be sacrilege to mention famous upland areas and not talk about the largest stretch of heather-coated moor in Britain. Every year between August and September, this otherwise grey-brown bracken-swathed high ground explodes with lilac hues as the flowers blossom. But it's not just the North York Moors' annual purple haze that makes it worth a visit. The area is also home to a supply of bilberries (good for foragers) – not to mention archaeological evidence dating back to 8,000BC. The North York Moors also boast limestone belts, forest and coast and even has a dale known as Great Fryup – surely the best place in the world to take the pan and have an alfresco brekkie.

↑ Whether visiting during the annual explosion of purple (lavender season) or not, the North York Moors National Park is a tasty moorland morsel

# *THE* RECIPES

# CAMPER'S HACK:

To make into a truly hearty meal,
serve with Bannock Bread (page 94).

## ·BREAKFAST·

## ⇒ ONE-PAN FRY-UP FOR ONE ⇐

*Nothing beats a greasy full English/Welsh/Scottish/Irish
to set you up after or before a full day's
tramping on the moorland. Here's how to make
the perfect one-pan pick-me-up.*

## INGREDIENTS

Knob of butter or splash of oil

2 chipolata sausages

2 rashers smoked back bacon

Handful of mushrooms, sliced

Handful of cherry tomatoes, halved

3 eggs, lightly beaten

Handful of grated cheese

1 garlic clove, chopped

## HERE'S THE PLAN ...

1. Turn on the camping stove and place a pan over the flame. Add the butter or oil and swirl the pan until it starts to sizzle.

2. Fry the sausages until they start to brown a little, 3–4 minutes, then add the bacon. Turn both continuously until the bacon becomes a little crispy, 4–5 minutes.

3. Add the mushrooms and tomatoes and carry on cooking until everything looks almost ready to eat, 3–5 minutes usually.

4. Drain off any remaining fat then spread out all the ingredients and add the egg, making sure it completely covers the pan so there are no gaps between breakfast items.

5. As the egg starts to set (a couple of minutes should suffice) add the cheese and garlic. Continue cooking for another couple of minutes.

6. Either eat straight from the pan if you're lacking in plates or consider cutting up into slices (you could always save some for lunch).

·BREAKFAST·

# ⇒ SPICED HOT APPLE GRANOLA ⇐

*For those who prefer to skip the fry-up, this healthier
fruit-filled option quite literally spices up a bowl of
granola and combines both quick-release sugar
with slow-burn grains and apple.*

## INGREDIENTS

1 eating apple (I like Granny Smith or Golden
  Delicious)

Brown sugar, to taste

Pinch of ground cinnamon (optional)

Knob of butter

Cupful of granola

Handful of raisins or blueberries

## HERE'S THE PLAN ...

1. Core, then slice and dice the apple.

2. Place the diced apple in a sealable, reusable plastic food bag with the sugar and cinnamon,
   if using. Shake until the apple chunks are covered.

3. Turn on the camping stove and heat up a pan, add the butter and heat until it starts to
   bubble. Throw in the apple along with about four sporkfuls of water and gently heat for
   around 10 minutes. The apple will start to soften – don't let it warm for so long that it turns
   into sauce!

4. Drain off any excess water. Stir in the granola and fruit with an extra pinch of cinnamon, if
   desired and pour into a cup or bowl or, of course, eat straight from the pan.

# ⇒ BANANA SAVOURY ⇐

*For slow-release energy and to help heal tired muscles you can't beat a banana. But it doesn't have to be a dessert. Add some peanuts and heat for a quick and unexpected savoury boost.*

## INGREDIENTS

1 ripe banana

2 sporkfuls of smooth peanut butter

Handful of salted peanuts

**Plus** Foil

## HERE'S THE PLAN …

1. Slice the unpeeled banana, through the skin, along one side.
2. Fill the gap with the peanut butter, then scatter over the peanuts.
3. Wrap the banana in foil and if you have a metal spork or utensil heat over the camp stove flame or place directly in the flame of a Kelly Kettle (page 20). Leave for about 10 minutes, turning frequently, and checking halfway through.
4. When the skin starts to blacken, the inside is usually perfect. Dig in and enjoy!

## ⇌ PESTO POLENTA ⇌

*Handily often pre-made into a loaf-like structure,
this cornmeal dish will give you tons of tasty
slow-release energy. Served with pesto and cheese it's a
true slice of comfort to enjoy high on the moors!*

## INGREDIENTS

½ x 500g pack of ready cooked polenta
  (available from supermarkets)
Knob of butter
100g green pesto

Handful of grated cheese
Cooked stinging nettle leaves (optional;
  page 185)

## HERE'S THE PLAN ...

1. Cut the polenta into slices, approximately 1.5–2cm thick (too thin and they won't cook properly).
2. Turn on the camping stove and heat up a frying pan (it needs to be large enough to hold the polenta slices in a single layer), add the butter and heat until it starts to bubble.
3. Carefully add the polenta slices, laying them flat in the pan and cook for 8–10 minutes per side. Although it's tempting to keep checking – resist the urge to flip them as they need at least 8 minutes each side to cook properly, turning too soon will break them up.
4. Once both sides have done their time serve by drizzling with pesto, sprinkling with cheese and, for the brave, garnishing with your pre-prepared stinging nettle leaves.

## CAMPER'S HACK:

Beef mince can be used in place of the quorn. Consider pre-freezing the mince at home and letting it defrost while you hike your way to your chosen overnight venue.

# · D I N N E R ·

## ⇒ QUORN COWBOY CHILLI ⇐

*Packed full of protein – this meat-free hot dish
will refuel the fire after a long day spent
heather and bog bashing.*

## INGREDIENTS

Knob of butter or splash of oil

100g Quorn mince (can substitute with meat
if desired)

2 mini-peppers or 1 regular pepper,
deseeded and sliced

½ x 415g can Heinz Five Beans

Dash of Tabasco sauce

Pinch of paprika

1 x 30g bag of tortilla chips

## HERE'S THE PLAN ...

1. Turn on the camping stove and heat the butter or oil in a frying pan.

2. Once the butter or oil is sizzling, throw in the Quorn and cook until it starts to brown nicely,
around 5 minutes, stirring occasionally.

3. When the mince is browned, add the pepper slices and stir for a couple of minutes until
they start to soften.

4. Add the beans, Tabasco and paprika and stir well. Simmer for 4–5 minutes or until the
beans are heated through and bubbling slowly.

5. To serve, pour the chilli into your camping bowl. Crush the tortilla chips while still in their
bag, then open and sprinkle over the chilli.

·DINNER·

# ⇌ AMAZING AUBERGINE ⇌

*Easy and quick to make, this tasty dish will replenish the calories in no time, while being a little lighter on the stomach, so a good option if preparing later in the evening.*

## INGREDIENTS

1 aubergine
Handful of breadcrumbs

1 egg
Splash of oil

## HERE'S THE PLAN ...

1. Wait until you are about to cook before preparing the aubergine as it will brown very quickly. When you're ready, trim and slice it into 1cm discs.
2. Place the breadcrumbs on a plate. Crack the egg into a cup or bowl and beat with a spork.
3. Turn on the camping stove and heat some oil in a frying pan, to a depth of about 3mm. Once the oil begins to bubble take a disc of aubergine and dip it first in the egg then the breadcrumbs to coat. Then place it in the pan.
4. Repeat for all the discs until you've filled the base of the pan.
5. Cook the discs for about 4 minutes, turning frequently until both sides are golden and beginning to brown. Serve and enjoy!

# ⇒ BBQ BEANS ⇐

*Mixing sweet and savoury flavours with some energy-packed superfoods means that even those not keen on regular baked beans will love these souped-up variants.*

## INGREDIENTS

Knob of butter or splash of oil

1 small onion or shallot, chopped

1 garlic clove, sliced

Splash of malt vinegar

1 sporkful of brown sugar

½ x 400g can pinto beans, drained

1 x 200g pack of tomato passata

1 sporkful of black treacle (optional)

## HERE'S THE PLAN ...

1. Fire up the camping stove, add the butter or oil to a pan and heat until it starts to bubble. Add the onion or shallot and fry until it starts to brown.

2. Add the garlic and fry for another 1–2 minutes – making sure the onion doesn't burn, reduce the heat if necessary.

3. Next pop in a splash of vinegar and the brown sugar and heat until the sugar has dissolved and the vinegar has reduced to coat the onions and garlic.

4. Now add the beans and stir in the passata. For a truly sumptuous snack add a spoonful of black syrup and stir in to add some rich sweetness to the flavour, heating gently. Serve straight from the pan.

## CAMPER'S HACK:

Key for this recipe is to have a container you can leave the mix in to 'set' when it's done. I find a mess tin is best for this, but any rectangular plastic food box or similar will do the job. Have this clean and ready before you start.

·SNACKS·

# ⇒ NO-BAKE FLAPJACK ⇐

*Whether you opt to make this at home before your trip*
*(it's a great last-minute one as it is so quick to make),*
*or decide to make at your campsite, this moreish*
*flapjack is sure to sustain you.*

## INGREDIENTS

100g rolled porridge oats

50g puffed rice breakfast cereal

100g dried cranberries

50g hazelnuts

50g sesame seeds

Knob of butter

100g light brown or muscovado sugar

200g golden syrup

**Plus** Mess tin with lid or reusable plastic
food box with lid

## HERE'S THE PLAN ...

1. Put the porridge oats, rice cereal and cranberries in the container and mix together as best you can.

2. Fire up the camping stove and heat a frying pan over a medium flame, add the hazelnuts and sesame seeds and warm gently until they are toasted. Remove the pan from the heat, let them cool then add them to the container and mix together.

3. Add the butter to the now empty pan along with the sugar and syrup, heating until it becomes a thick and drizzly consistency.

4. Without delay, take the pan off the heat and immediately pour the mixture into the container. Mix so that everything is covered with the syrup (you will need to move fast) then press down firmly so that the rectangular shape is formed. Cover and set aside.

5. In theory you could eat this immediately, but it's much nicer to let it cool for around 3 hours or more first. If at home making pre-trip, pop it in the fridge. If camping, cover with a lid (you do not want any midges getting into this mixture as they will stick to it!) and leave it in your porch overnight to cool ready for the next day's walk.

# CAMPER'S HACK:

Dried milk powder rehydrated with water can be used for longer trips.

## ⇥ MALTED MILK DRINK ⇤

*Sometimes, after a hard day's walk,*
*all it takes is a hot drink to help you feel right again.*
*Make this malted option – with a healthy dose of*
*Maltesers for the perfect winter warmer.*

## INGREDIENTS

1 pint carton full-fat milk
½ x 397g can Nestlé Carnation Caramel

1 x 25g sachet Ovaltine or Horlicks
Handful of Maltesers

## HERE'S THE PLAN ...

1. A nice and easy pre-bed tipple. Turn on the camping stove and pour the milk into a pan and heat steadily over a medium flame.

2. Add the Carnation Caramel and stir constantly (this has the tendency to congeal so stir thoroughly as it warms up). When smooth and well combined take off the heat.

3. Empty the sachet of Ovaltine into a mug and pour the heated milk mixture on top. Stir thoroughly while pouring and keep stirring for a couple of minutes afterwards.

4. Top with a handful of Maltesers and drink. Be prepared for a slight sugar high!

# ⇒ PEANUT BUTTER & FLAXSEED TRUFFLES ⇐

*Forget your boxes of fancy chocolates,*
*to make a fuel-laden sweet that will keep you going for*
*another day's adventure, then you need to make your*
*own treats. Make before you go, on the move*
*on the moors or even in the car.*

## INGREDIENTS

250g smooth peanut butter

1 ripe banana, chopped

200g porridge oats

75g flax seeds, crushed

85g mini-chocolate chips

1 x 25g sachet cocoa powder

**Plus** Plastic food box with lid or greaseproof
paper

## HERE'S THE PLAN ...

1. Put all the ingredients into a camping bowl and stir well so that they stick together.

2. Cover and leave somewhere cool for at least 30 minutes. If camping, then you could cover
and place the container (secure and well sealed) in a stream to chill it.

3. After waiting as long as you can, retrieve the mixture and use your fingers to roll the mixture
into 5cm balls.

4. To keep the truffles fresh put in a reusable plastic food box with lid or wrap in greaseproof
paper and enjoy for several days in the wild.

# COAST

Land's End in Cornwall epitomises the wonderfully rugged British coastline (SS)

**W**hite horses dashed towards me from the horizon, galloping over the sand in their frothy wake. I was fifteen. My friend was talking to me about the kind of nonsense that seems important when you are an angsty teenager. But I heard none of it. Instead, stood on a promenade on the North Wales coast, I was mesmerised by the sheer power of the waves.

It wasn't like this was the first time I had ever seen the ocean. When I was a child we moved from inland England to a Welsh town just above the sea. Although some distance away, I could see waves from my bedroom window. The sea provided the backdrop to many a childhood adventure – as it does for many of us who live on our little island of Britain.

My granny would take me to the beach in the summer holidays, where we built sandcastles and peered into rock pools when the tide went out. On stormy days, after she finished work, my mum would drive my brother and me, right up to the edge of the local breakwater so we could feel the spray of the turbulent sea and watch, awestruck, its remarkable power. My dad even taught me to ride my bike alongside the winding coast.

And yet, despite the sea appearing in most photos from those early years, I don't believe I'd ever truly noticed it until that teenage day. Suddenly everything that I thought important seemed to pale and disappear. The might of the coast was manifest not merely in its physical strength, but also in its pull on my mind and its demand on my attention.

Even though, as an adult, work has taken me away from the sea, I've always found myself drawn back to it – no matter where I find myself. Whenever the opportunity arises to return, I grab it.

*"The sea provided the backdrop to many a childhood adventure"*

PHOEBE SMITH

As I approach the coast, I feel excitement rise from my belly. It is as though something inside me can sense when the sea is nearby.

I love to walk along the coast, to hear the waves crash against the stones, pulling them in and out from the shoreline in an endless cycle. I like to just watch the sea, recapturing the reverence I felt when I was a teen. But, perhaps most of all, I adore visiting new sections of the coast and camping wild there.

Although approaches to measuring coastlines vary, the UK's coastline extends for around 17,800km, which makes it longer than the seafront of Brazil and even India). Moreover, the British coastline offers diversity unrivalled by any other country. We have headlands, bays, islands, peninsulas, cliffs, shale spits, a Jurassic Coast and 43 designated Heritage coasts.

To the southeast are the chalky downs, the sheer white cliff faces of the Seven Sisters, and the flattened and sprawling estuaries, creeks and mudflats of Essex. To the southwest lie the bustling harbours of Portsmouth and Southampton, the fossil-rich pickings

↑ Traversing the Valley of the Rocks near Lynton, Exmoor

# FORAGE

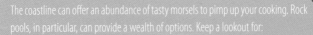

The coastline can offer an abundance of tasty morsels to pimp up your cooking. Rock pools, in particular, can provide a wealth of options. Keep a lookout for:

MUSSELS: these dark blue-black wedge-like shells are seen everywhere on the rocks found on British beaches, usually from October to March. Don't eat any with broken shells. Also avoid any that don't close when tapped, as they are dead. Thoroughly wash the mussels, then ideally steam them by adding some water or wine to a pan and heating for around 4–5 minutes. Avoid any ones that do not fully open after cooking.

COCKLES: the archetypal shell, coloured white or cream with indented ridges. These offer less meat than mussels, but can be found year-round. The paler the shell, the better. Soak in cold water for a few hours then boil or steam them to cook for 4–5 minutes until they open. Discard any that don't open.

SEAWEED: there's a huge range of seaweed on offer on our shores and, thankfully, there are no poisonous varieties. For something to use as a garnish, look for gutweed in spring. This is a very green cluster of thin tubes that look like a straggly moss. Rinse out sand, dry using your fleece or similar then fry for a crispy treat.

KELP: these very commonly seen brown, long ribbons can be added to soup or stews for flavour. Simply wash them thoroughly before adding to your dish to simmer for at least 15 minutes. Remove before serving.

DULSE: a brownish/purple sea vegetable that can be used like cabbage. Pick from December to July, wash thoroughly before use. It is particularly good in a stir-fry.

STOMPING GIRL/S

## KNOW YOUR TIDES

**TOP TIP**

If heading out to walk, camp or cook along the coast it's important that you don't put yourself at unnecessary risk by getting cut off by high tides or – worse still – woken in the night by waves crashing into your tent. So you don't get caught out, remember the following:

* Tide times and height change throughout the month: don't assume that if somewhere was easy to access one day it will be so the next.
* You can easily check before you go: tide tables are available from ⊘ tidetimes. org.uk, on the BBC website at ⊘ tinyurl.com/tide-BBC, via smartphone apps (eg: My Tide Times UK and Tides Planner), or by simply asking the local tourist office, Royal National Lifeboat Institution lifeguards or harbour masters, or checking details displayed in various local seaside shops.
* Be aware when there: always keep a close eye on the direction and speed of the tide. If you're unsure about whether or not a place will be cut off, don't risk it.

Cornwall's Bedruthan steps – lovely to look at (and cook among) but do check tides before heading down to the sand (LUKASZ PAJOR/S)

> *"What the coast lacks in terms of potable water, it makes up for in foraging potential"*

of Dorset and the Isle of Wight, and the wooded valleys and historic fishing hamlets of Cornwall (replete with hidden coves and caves that whisper of a smuggling past). Heading slightly north there's the drama of Exmoor with soaring cliffs shaped like castles, which cede to the expansive Bristol Channel.

Then comes Wales which houses the rugged majesty of the Pembrokeshire coast, the golden sands of mid-Wales and the surfers' paradise of the Llyn Peninsula, not to mention the Victorian promenades of the northern coast. Northern England continues with 'old-skool' beachside fare, Antony Gormley's lifelike statues looking out to sea at Crosby, intermixed with the cockle-picking flats of Morecambe Bay and the Cumbria coast beyond.

Scotland raises the bar with a mix of fjord-like lochs on the western coast, giving way to sea cliffs and promontories, islands, and sandy bays – many of the last giving the Caribbean a run for its money. Scotland's northern coast is a wild, rugged and bird-covered sanctuary, while its low-lying eastern flank offers the expansive sands of estuaries, firths and nature reserves.

Proceeding south along the North Sea edge, northeast England offers bustling cites betwixt windswept silt, towering cliffs and the Humber Estuary, not to mention shingle, chalk and Northumberland's Holy Island of Lindisfarne. Finally, step forward Norfolk and Suffolk, home of big skies, striped cliffs, marshy estuaries and nature reserves. In short, Britain is home to an embarrassment of coastal riches – all of which are no more than 113km (70 miles) away, wherever we may live.

Cooking and camping by the sea offers not only variety in scenery, but also in food. You have to be inventive: you may be surrounded by water yet none of it is drinkable (unless you somehow have a desalinator). So carrying your own drinking water or sourcing from rivers en route is mandatory. But then what the coast lacks in terms of potable water, it makes up for in foraging potential – from fish to seaweed, shellfish to crabs (see *Forage*, page 77). And then, of course, there is the very real delight – no less tasty than the best meal – of simply stopping conversation and staring at the might of the ocean.

The stop-conversation-in-its-tracks beauty of Lindisfarne ↑

# ≡ SECRET INGREDIENTS ≡

*Once you have your grub sorted, it's time to locate the best patches of prime natural seaside real estate in which to get your coastal kicks ...*

## 1. LLANDDWYN ISLAND, ANGLESEY, NORTH WALES

When it comes to love – whether that be for another person, food or the great outdoors itself – there is no better location than this 'isle on an isle', which was home to none other than St Dwynwen – the Welsh patron saint of lovers. Legend has it that when she was denied her love she opted for a hermit's life on this particular stretch of the Welsh coastline. When you start cooking here, perhaps take a minute to remember the saint, before falling head over heels for the location yourself.

## 2. LUSKENTYRE SANDS, ISLE OF HARRIS, SCOTLAND

There was a time when only a handful of lucky folk were even aware of the existence of this Outer Hebridean sandy strip. However, social media (and guidebooks, admittedly) have a wonderful way of spreading the word and now this far-flung piece of paradise is

Lovely Llanddwyn Island, Angelsey (HELEN HOTSON/S)

on many a wish list. Given its remoteness, however, it still is far from crowded, and the sand is so white and the sea so blue that by the time you do make it here to camp you will likely need to pinch yourself to check you're not actually dreaming …

## 3. BLAKENEY, NORFOLK, ENGLAND

The north Norfolk coast is many things to many people. To the Hunstanton crowd it's home to fish and chips, sticks of rock and candy-striped deckchairs. To the Holme crowd it's a twitcher's dream, being slap bang on the migration route for many a winged species. But for a wilderness lover it's all about Blakeney Point. Hemmed in from the sea by salt marshes it feels far removed from just about anywhere. The highlight is the shingle spit of Blakeney Point, which (between November and early January) provides a home to calving grey seals that collectively produce over 2,000 pups each year.

NEIL BURTON/S

↑ The gorgeous greys of Blakeney Point, Norfolk

GRAHAM HUNT/A

## 4. WORBARROW BAY, DORSET, ENGLAND

Slightly east of the deservedly headline-grabbing beauty of Durdle Door and Lulworth Cove on Purbeck's fossil-laden Jurassic Coast is a stretch of coast that is not always accessible, for the Army grants access only intermittently. Home to the now ghost-village of Tyneham – which was occupied by the military in World War II and never returned to its residents – there remains an allure about this now-abandoned stretch of waterfront. Moreover, due to the lack of farming, it has almost become wilder than anywhere else.

## 5. WALBERSWICK BEACH, SUFFOLK, ENGLAND

Bordered by heath, marshland and a nature reserve of the same name, this shingle beach is perfect for those who like a spot of nature with their cooking. With a plethora of sand dunes to tuck yourself into, privacy is virtually guaranteed. And as Walberswick is also famous for crabbing, if you're up for it, a sea-inspired extra ingredient could well be on the cards.

The mysterious, often out-of-bounds Worbarrow Bay on the Jurassic Coast ↑

## 6. ARNSIDE & SILVERDALE, LANCASHIRE/CUMBRIA, ENGLAND

Sitting as they do above Morecambe Bay, yet below the boundaries of the Lake District National Park, the coastal cliffs that make up this area are pretty much overlooked by most. But wilderness lovers rejoice: here you can easily find a secluded spot, whether sat on clifftops or limestone outcrops above the sea, or watching birdlife swarm around the Kent Estuary. For this is one coastal hideaway to which grockles – thankfully – are not partial.

## 7. ROBIN HOOD'S BAY, NORTH YORKSHIRE, ENGLAND

A few miles south of Britain's first proper seaside town, Whitby, lies a short stretch of cliff-hewn sand that was named after the famous folk hero who stole from the rich to give to the poor. With rocks dating back to the Jurassic period, this is the place where fossils, footprints from dinosaurs and ammonites are often found. Then there are the rock pools – nature's larder of potential added extras for your feast.

## 8. REDPOINT BEACH, WESTER ROSS, SCOTLAND

Sat – quite literally – at the end of the road, this remote beach (which does – surprise, surprise – have very reddish-pink sand) is a wilderness banquet. From sand dunes to grassland, views over The Minch to the Isle of Skye, and the possibility of following the adjacent footpath all the way to Torridon without passing another town (a journey that would take hours by car), Redpoint is a beach destined to be explored. But don't rush it. Take out your stove, drink in your surrounds among the many piles of middens (waste from early human occupation) and relax.

# A DRIFTWOOD DEN

Fancy building a little makeshift shelter that blends in your surrounds much better than a tent or bivvy? If so, the following steps should help:

1. Patrol the beach looking for driftwood. Chunks that have been washed up (but have not been dragged out again by the tide) usually lie around the high-tide mark.

2. Collect a selection of sizes. You will need a fair bit to make a shelter the length of your body and shorter pieces of wood for the 'walls'.

3. Find an area well clear of potential rockfall then start by erecting the shelter entrance by placing two shorter pieces together to form a triangle (the ground being the third 'side'), remembering that they need to be long enough so that when leaning together you can fit underneath them still. Then rest the longest piece – the length of your body – between the entrance triangle and stick it deep into the sand.

4. Use shorter pieces to form the 'wall' and cover this with grass to help plug the gaps. You may wish to add larger rocks at either end to help with stability.

5. Put your camping mat and sleeping bag inside the shelter, placing your head at the entrance, and enjoy a cosy night's sleep. Zzzzz . . .

PHOEBE SMITH

The practice of making dens at Peppercombe Beach in North Devon has been a tradition for many years ↑

# 9. TRÀIGH NA H-UAMHAG, HIGHLAND, SCOTLAND

This is one beach that you won't find listed on many websites. If driving along the newly hip 'North Coast 500' route in Scotland (⌀ northcoast500.com) – that's the A836 to you and me – this is a 'blink-and-you-miss-it' piece of gold (literally the colour of the sand!) Sat in front of Scotland's most northerly Munro (a hill of at least 3,000 feet or 914m) of Ben Hope, this little patch of sand hides caves and jagged rocky protrusions that look like giant underground sea creatures, and gives views of some of the best sunsets in the world.

# 10. FRESHWATER WEST BEACH, PEMBROKESHIRE, WALES

It's not often that you see a location in a Hollywood franchise and arrive to find that not only is it as breathtakingly beautiful in real life (without any CGI special effects), but actually is even more 'A-list' than you ever thought possible. Fringing West Pembrokeshire coastline is this yawning stretch of golden sand. It is most famous, perhaps, for the backdrop it provided in *Harry Potter and the Deathly Hallows*. But when you visit, the only celebrity is the coastal scenery itself.

↑ Freshwater West was home to the Shell House and resting place to free elf Dobbie in the Harry Potter films

# THE RECIPES

# ·BREAKFAST·

## ⇒ TOASTED EGG NEST ⇐

*Cut a hole in your bread to use it to contain the perfect egg while it cooks – a protein-rich start to the day.*

## INGREDIENTS

1 slice of bread

Knob of butter or splash of oil

1 egg

Black pepper

## HERE'S THE PLAN ...

1. Using the knife-edge of your spork cut a roughly circular hole in the centre of the slice of bread.

2. Turn on the camping stove and heat the butter or oil in a frying pan until it starts to bubble.

3. Lay the slice of bread in the pan and immediately break the egg into the hole — trying to keep the yolk whole. Cook on a medium heat for about 1 minute — or until the egg white has begun to set, then flip it over.

4. Let it cook for another 1–2 minutes, moving it occasionally to stop the egg sticking to the frying pan.

5. Flip again to ensure both sides are evenly cooked. Once the bread has started to brown and the egg white has set it's ready to eat. Add a sprinkle of black pepper and serve immediately.

## CAMPER'S HACK:

Before you leave home, wrap your bread in foil and pack it at the top of your rucksack to stop it getting squashed.

# ⇒ LEMON & CINNAMON MUFFINS ⇐

*Get your campfire going and start your day the sweeter (and sour) way, with a muffin cooked inside the fruit itself for a tasty treat with novelty factor.*

## INGREDIENTS

4 small lemons
1 packet sponge cake mix
1 egg

Pinch of ground cinnamon
**Plus** Foil

## HERE'S THE PLAN ...

1. Cut the top off each lemon (keep the lids to one side, for later) and, using a spoon or spork, remove all the flesh from inside the fruit and put it in a bowl.

2. Remove the seeds and white pith and discard them responsibly. Put the carved-out lemons to one side, for later.

3. Add the cake mix to the bowl of lemon with the egg, cinnamon and 100ml water. Mix well, until it is smooth (barring the lemon bits).

4. Pour the mixture into each of the lemon shells, they should be about two-thirds full.

5. Replace the lids and wrap each lemon in foil. Place on to the campfire, turning regularly.

6. Depending on how hot the fire is, they should be ready to eat in 20 minutes but do check after 10 minutes by sticking your spork in – if they're ready no mixture should stick to it as you pull it out. Remove the lids and enjoy!

## CAMPER'S HACK:

Some supermarkets sell sundried tomato or cheese bread mix where all you have to do is add water. Buy one of these if you prefer, follow the pack instructions to make the dough and then knead in the tomatoes and cook as opposite, from step 3.

## ⇌ SUNDRIED TOMATO BANNOCK BREAD ⇌

*Make a campfire classic with an added
tomato twist for a fantastic shared
accompaniment or a one-man meal in itself.*

## INGREDIENTS

300g plain flour
100g powdered milk
1 tsp baking power

Handful of sundried tomatoes, drained of oil
1 tsp oil or a knob of butter

## HERE'S THE PLAN ...

1. Place the flour, powdered milk and baking powder in a bowl and gradually add just enough water to form a soft dough. It should just hold together without being too sticky.

2. Add the sundried tomatoes and knead the dough for at least 5 minutes.

3. Turn on the camping stove, add the oil or butter to a frying pan and heat until it starts to bubble. Place the dough in the pan to form a round, 3cm thick, bread. Depending on the size of the pan, you may need to cook the bread in batches.

4. Cook the bread on a low-medium heat on the camping stove or by placing the pan directly on to the embers of a campfire, rotating the bread in the pan every few minutes to ensure it cooks evenly and doesn't stick to the pan.

5. Turn over and continue to rotate on this side. Cooking time will be around 10–15 minutes but can vary depending on your stove – it should look loaf like and start to crack. Tap on it and when it sounds hollow it's cooked.

6. Remove from the heat and the pan, place on a rock and allow to cool before eating.

## ⇒ CAMPING QUESADILLAS ⇐

*Get in touch with your Mexican side with a celebratory –
and cheese-laden – midday masterpiece.*

### INGREDIENTS

Knob of butter or splash of oil

2 tortillas

Handful of grated Cheddar, red Leicester or
Mexicana® cheese

### HERE'S THE PLAN ...

1. Turn on the camping stove and heat half the butter or oil in a frying pan until it starts to
   bubble. Add one tortilla and fry for 2 minutes, on one side only. Place the cooked tortilla on
   a plate.

2. Heat the remaining butter or oil in the pan and add the uncooked tortilla. Sprinkle the
   cheese over the tortilla in the pan and top with the cooked tortilla, soft side down.

3. Using a spork or spatula press the tortillas together and cook over a medium heat until the
   cheese begins to melt. Flip the tortillas over and cook for a minute or so; remove from the
   heat, slice and serve.

## ⇌ TOMATO & HALLOUMI KEBABS ⇌

*Give yourself a hearty dose of greens, and reds and purples with these campfire-roasted sumptuous skewers.*

## INGREDIENTS

1 small aubergine

1 small courgette

Handful cherry tomatoes

100g halloumi cheese, cut into large cubes

1 tbsp clear honey

Splash of oil

Splash of lemon juice

**Plus** Wire rack

## HERE'S THE PLAN ...

1. First find four wooden sticks suitable for cooking – the best will be thin but strong. Soak these in water for about 30 minutes to stop them burning on the campfire.

2. Turn on the camping stove and bring a pan of water to the boil. Trim and slice the aubergine and courgette and add to the boiling water. Simmer for about 5 minutes or so until soft and then drain.

3. Thread the vegetable slices, whole cherry tomatoes and halloumi cubes on to the soaked wooden sticks.

4. Mix the honey with a dash of oil and cover the vegetables with it.

5. For the halloumi, mix the oil with the lemon juice and dip the edges in it so that it browns with a tasty zing.

6. Place a wire rack over a campfire or Kelly Kettle, and put the kebabs on the flames. Turn frequently so they cook evenly. When nicely browned, serve.

## CAMPER'S HACK:

Combine tandoori paste, chilli, paprika, coriander, honey and lemon juice before you leave home and transport them in a reusable plastic storage container or bag.

## ⇒ TANDOORI SALMON ⇐

*Once you have your campfire going, spice up a canned classic with a spot of chilli and spices – you'll literally be swimming in flavour.*

## INGREDIENTS

1 x 105g can MSC-certified red salmon
1 tbsp tandoori paste
Pinch of chilli powder
1 tsp smoked paprika
Pinch of ground coriander

½ tsp clear honey
Splash of lemon juice
Single-portion pack of boil-in-the-bag rice
**Plus** Foil

## HERE'S THE PLAN …

1. Open the can of salmon and drain off the excess liquid.

2. In a bowl mix the tandoori paste with the chilli, paprika, coriander, honey and lemon juice to form a thick paste.

3. Spoon half the paste on to a piece of foil and place the salmon on top. Spoon the remaining curry mixture on top of the salmon, to cover it completely.

4. Turn on the camping stove and cook the boil-in-the-bag rice, following the pack instructions.

5. Wrap the salmon up in the foil and place in the fire for about 5 minutes. Turn the parcel over and cook for a further 4–5 minutes.

6. Drain the cooked rice. Check the salmon is hot all the way through and serve over the rice.

# ·SNACKS·

## ⇒ SPICED HUSKY CORN ⇐

*Cooked on a campfire or a Kelly Kettle,
corn on the cob just got a makeover – foil and
skewers not even required!*

## INGREDIENTS

2 corn on the cobs, in husks
Knob of butter

Pinch of paprika

## HERE'S THE PLAN ...

1. Peel the husks back on the corn and remove all the silk, leaving the large green leaves. Soak the corn in cold water for about 20 minutes.

2. Remove from the water and shake or sit in the sunshine (if available) to dry.

3. Turn on the camping stove and heat the butter in a small pan until melted. Stir in the paprika.

4. Coat the corn with the paprika butter and replace the husks.

5. Place the corn directly on to the hot ashes of a campfire or on the wire rack of a Kelly Kettle and turn frequently for around 15 minutes or until tender. Peel back the husks — and use instead of skewers to prevent burnt fingers!

# ⇌ SWEET CINNAMON BREADSTICKS ⇌

*A literal twist on campfire-cooked damper bread,
certain to make your mouth water.*

## INGREDIENTS

350g self-raising flour
1 tbsp butter
2 tbsp milk powder

1 tsp sugar
Pinch of cinnamon
Pinch of salt

## HERE'S THE PLAN ...

1. Find pieces of wood, which would serve well for the bread to be twisted around — around 3–4cm in diameter. Strip them of their bark and set them aside.

2. Mix all the ingredients together in a bowl and add water gradually to form a dough. It should bind together well without being too sticky. Roll the dough out using hands to form snake-like strips no more than about 30cm long each.

3. Heat the sticks over the campfire or stove flame for a couple of minutes to warm them up, but do not let them burn.

4. Wrap the strips of dough around the warmed sticks (twisted fashion) and hold over the flame turning regularly so that they cook evenly. After around 5–10 minutes they will be browned nicely and ready to eat — fresh and warm.

## CAMPER'S HACK:

Go for dark chocolate digestives
if available to save on faff!

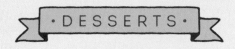

# · D E S S E R T S ·

## ⇒ BRITISH S'MORES ⇐

*The Brits' answer to the American graham cracker favourite – utterly calorie laden, irresistibly moreish.*

## INGREDIENTS

Dark chocolate (1 large cube per s'more)    Marshmallows (1–2 per s'more)
Digestive biscuit (2 per s'more)

## HERE'S THE PLAN ...

1. Find some thin sticks to use for toasting the marshmallows – peel the bark off the end with a sharp knife (always cutting away from your body).

2. Pop the biscuits and chocolate on a plate. Then load up your marshmallows on to the sticks – kebab-style.

3. Heat the marshmallows over a camping stove flame or campfire, turning frequently so that they brown well.

4. Slide the marshmallows on to a biscuit, add a slice of dark chocolate and complete the sandwich with another biscuit. Yummy!

# CAMPER'S HACK:

If pre-packed scone mix is unavailable,
use the ingredients for the *Sweet Cinnamon
Breadsticks* recipe (page 104)
minus cinnamon and follow from step 2.

## ⇒ CAMPFIRE TARTS ⇐

*Get creative with your puddings and use
a flask lid to create a sweet that
looks distinctly gourmet.*

## INGREDIENTS

¼ pack scone mix
1 tbsp milk powder
Knob of butter
1 small can sliced peaches

Whipped cream in a can (optional luxury
   treat)
**Plus** Lid of a stainless-steel flask or a
   stainless-steel camping cup

## HERE'S THE PLAN ...

1. Put the scone mix and milk powder into a bowl and gradually add enough water to form a dough that is pliable and not overly sticky.

2. Grease the outside of the stainless-steel flask lid with the butter, then wrap the dough around the outside of the lid. Don't make it too thick or too deep otherwise it will take too long to cook.

3. Hold the lid, by placing it on a thick stick, over a campfire flame, rotating frequently, for a few minutes, until the dough turns golden.

4. Remove the cooked tart from the lid. Drain the peaches. Fill the tart with some peaches, and serve, with cream, if available.

# MOUNTAIN

Buachaille Etive Mòr – the archetypal mountain of Britain (SS)

I t is hard to accurately describe what it is like to stand looking down on the clouds without gushing profusely in a stream of unbridled adjectives. Most of us have been in planes so have experienced the sensation of sitting in a (sort of) comfy chair at 35,000 feet (10,660m) and looking at the big fluffy white blanket of cumulus vapours floating below. But that sight is experienced from within the confines of a metal box, drinking bad coffee, surrounded by the smells and sounds of a few hundred other souls, silently wishing that the whole ordeal will be over very quickly.

Climb a mountain (or even a small hill), however, and wake up on the very top as the only person for miles and it is a different experience entirely. With a cup of freshly brewed tea in one hand, a bowl of steaming porridge in the other, and nothing but clouds stretching out just inches from your feet it is, I believe, as close to heaven on earth as you can get.

I will never forget my first cloud inversion. This is a delightful mountain phenomenon where – in a total twist of the natural order – the tops of the mountains are warmer than the lower slopes, with cold air trapped in valleys under a layer of fog or cloud. I had seen hundreds of photos of cloud inversions before and always thought them mind-blowingly beautiful. But it wasn't until I was walking up Ben Nevis one icy winter morning, having been forced by freezing fog to camp at the lochan halfway up its flanks, when I finally saw one with my own eyes.

Popping out of the mist, I was suddenly confronted by a view that rivalled any that I had seen in my life – and, indeed, rivals any I have seen since. Distant mountain tops poked out of the cloud as though islands were emerging from a creamy and wispy sea.

*"Wake up on the very top as the only person for miles"*

Sitting above the clouds during an inversion on Ben Nevis –
the perfect place for a much-needed snack (PHOEBE SMITH)

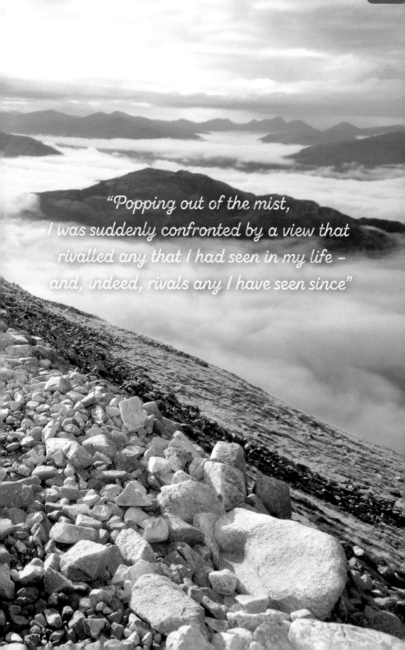

"Popping out of the mist,
I was suddenly confronted by a view that
rivalled any that I had seen in my life –
and, indeed, rivals any I have seen since"

## COOKING IN HIGH WINDS

On mountains, strong winds (and not just from those feasting on curry) can be an issue. Flames may go out, may not heat evenly or may not even light at all. Don't be tempted to take the stove inside your tent, though, no matter what; it's not worth the risk of carbon monoxide poisoning. Instead, look for natural shelters – rocks, and even your body can provide a windbreak to get the flame going. If there are rocks, build a mini-windbreak with them or even consider burying your stove slightly to take it out of the wind's reach.

The light seemed clearer and almost pink. Despite the temperature remaining low, I no longer felt cold.

Perhaps it is a burning need to witness more of these always elusive and quite unpredictable inversions that takes me back to the mountains time and time again. I have seen many more since – at dawn, at dusk, and even in the middle of the day. I've looked upon the ring of a Brocken spectre – when your shadow is cast on clouds with a rainbow halo (known as a 'glory') appearing around your head. I have observed a 'fogbow' (or white rainbow) emerge over the peaks. And I have gazed upon a blood moon so close that I swore I could reach out and touch it with my fingers.

Seeing these natural wonders is never guaranteed; moreover, the event is typically fleeting. I confess that this almost pleases me. Because not seeing them forces you to look at all the other reasons why standing on the top of any summit, of any height, communing with mountains and hills, is an experience that everyone should have at least once in their lives.

Hill-walking can be hard: when I began striding upwards, I felt ludicrously unfit and unwieldy. I plodded up slopes, breathing heavily, watching the top bob up and down, seemingly remaining an eternity away, thinking I would never reach it. But then that's most of the battle with mountains – the mental struggle. Just knowing you can do it makes the hike a thousand times easier. And when you pack your bag with the best kind of food to cook on your adventure … then it's easier still.

Ascending peaks means that anything you eat must sustain you: the hike is all about stamina rather than speed. Slow-release carbohydrates are your friends, sugar hits help when you feel beaten and tired, and warm, comforting dishes in the evening provide just reward for your ample effort. So never take a salad – it will not satisfy – and don't deny yourself little treats that act as motivators when your energy is waning.

In mountains, particularly if sleeping on summits, you cannot always rely on finding suitable water sources. So you need to either plan ahead and collect some en route (which means taking a suitable container) or carry what you need with you (which means that recipes should not rely too heavily on masses of liquid).

PAUL TOMKINS/VS

With views like this to be had in the hills, why wouldn't you head for them? ↑

## AN EMERGENCY KNIFE

Forgot your knife? No worries, here's how to make your own single-use cutter.

1. Look for suitable rock that will flake well – think slate, quartz or flint. You want a shard that already looks arrowhead-shaped so there's not too much work needed. Then select a larger rock (several times bigger) to act as a hammer.

2. Wear gloves to protect your hands and glasses (if you have them) to shield your eyes.

3. Find a solid, large flat rock and place upon it, facing upwards, the shard that will become a blade.

4. Strike the shard with the hammer stone several times until a piece flakes off. It may take several attempts, but you should be able to produce an edge that is sharp enough to help you chop food.

Bothies – those free-to-use mountain shelters left open for walkers – are a great hidden network in the hills. One advantage is that they usually have solid-fuel stoves, enabling you to cook some meals on a fire. Alternatively, they provide shelter for your camping stove if it's very windy.

Tempting though it may be, I suggest not staying inside the admittedly welcoming space of a building. To me, the sound of a camping stove bubbling away, while you are sat high in the sky with only birds for company, is perhaps the most calming audio there is. Couple that with the feeling of a belly replete with great food, and rarely do I feel more contented.

Appeasing your appetite is important. So too rewarding your body with the loving kindness of homemade nourishment. But never forget that the privilege of being in the mountains is, in itself, the most gratifying high in the world. And all the adjectives in the English language are inadequate to describe it.

Many bothies, like this one in Assynt, Scotland, offer respite in the mountains to cook out of the elements, and many have a wood-burning stove, which is useful for cooking some dishes (TOM RICHARDSON SCOTLAND/A)

# ═ SECRET INGREDIENTS ═

*Once you know what to
cook to fuel your body to
climb the mountains, which
peaks offer the best options for
dining venues? Here's a soupçon
of suitable spots to make each
dish utterly delightful.*

## 1. ST CATHERINE'S HILL, ISLE OF WIGHT, ENGLAND

Combining ocean views, a 14th-century relic and the thrill of
taking a ferry to 'climb' this mini-mountain, the chalky downs
above Chale Bay are mouth-wateringly attractive. This particular
high point is marked by a structure called St Catherine's Oratory –
a beacon (actually a medieval example of a lighthouse) ordered to
be built by the Church as penance after a local was found selling
wine destined for French monks. The Oratory is known on the
Isle of Wight as the 'pepper pot' or 'salt pot' – so is sure to suitably
season any meal you make.

## 2. NANTLLE RIDGE, GWYNEDD, WALES

Even those among us who are not aficionados of hill-walking
have heard of Snowdon. Each year, half a million visitors heave
themselves to the oft-crowded top of the highest peak in Wales.

PHOEBE SMITH

But the perfect place to enjoy a hearty meal has to be the unassuming ridge known as Nantlle, opposite Snowdon. Nantlle is formed by a string of summits. Although none of these passes the 750m mark, the climb is still an impressive undertaking. There are lots of idyllic spots to pitch a tent, to watch the crowds throng on the country's tallest mountain and to laugh smugly knowing that where you're eating, no reservations are required …

## 3. BEN NEVIS, HIGHLANDS, SCOTLAND

It may seem somewhat odd to recommend setting out to eat on the top of Scotland's Ben Nevis, a summit so notorious for its bad weather that a meteorological observatory once adorned it. However, look back a little further and you'll find that those hardy Victorians also built a hotel up here. You can still see the crumbled foundations of the dining room on the roof of the world (or Britain, at least). Head up there now and you may get an unrivalled view of the Scottish Highlands and out to Lochs Linnhe, Eil and Leven. Should the rain start to fall, you can retreat to the emergency shelter – actually higher than the summit itself – and enjoy your dinner at altitude.

The uncrowded Nantlle Ridge is the connoisseur's route of choice in Snowdonia ↑

## 4. GLASTONBURY TOR, SOMERSET, ENGLAND

OK, so it's not quite a mountain in terms of stature, but in terms of legend, this peak is ginormous. It is currently graced with the Grade-I-listed tower of St Michael's, a 14th-century stone iteration of the previous wooden structure that was built in the 11th century before being destroyed by an earthquake in 1275. Glastonbury Tor is the setting for many an Arthurian legend. Known as Ynys yr Afalon (Welsh for 'Isle of Avalon'), this is both the legendary resting place for King Arthur and Queen Guinevere and the location where Excalibur was forged. From the Tor's top it's easy to see why royalty and fable converged here, because the surrounding land drops off dramatically on all sides, slumping into what was once boggy marsh. Read the legends and imagine dragons circling above as you dine like a king.

## 5. BUNNET STANE, FIFE, SCOTLAND

Little known outside Scottish circles, this mushroom-like lump of sandstone is a novel formation in the smaller Lomond hills. Standing on a column of rock, weathered by the elements over millennia, it offers a platform around the size of a car roof from which to enjoy views of the surrounding countryside. Doing so might make you feel like a pixie in a fairytale, atop your own toadstool.

## FORAGE

Wild staples do not abound in the mountains. Easiest to identify and most common (not to mention very palatable) are bilberries (known as blaeberries in Scotland). Softer and juicier than the blueberries they resemble, they grow low, close to the ground on mountain flanks as well as in some Scots pine forests. Found between July and September they can help sweeten porridge or add to a dessert.

ZAK BENTLEY

If the weather turns, you can retreat to Maiden's Bower, a manmade cave that lies beneath the summit. It is said to have once been the home of a woman who fell in love with a rival family's son and refused to return when their marriage was denied. Happily you can be united with good food to make this a more palatable place to linger.

## 6. THE COBBLER, ARGYLL & BUTE, SCOTLAND

Distinctive and unmistakable, the mountain also known as Ben Arthur offers unrivalled views of the Arrochar Alps. Amid its three summits, the ultimate dining table can be found in the middle, marked by a distinct outcrop shaped remarkably like a buffet stand. To get on to it requires you to 'thread the needle', which essentially means crawling through a hole to reach a very exposed ledge before scrambling up to the top. The thought of tackling this may leave you sick to your stomach. The good news is that incredible views can be had even if you don't get to the top, and with the right food, you won't care whether or not you made the highest point.

A wild night hanging around at Bunnet Stane in Fife ↑

# 7. FAN BRYCHEINIOG, POWYS, WALES

Like many a peak in a national park, those that don't hold the accolade for being the biggest tend to miss out on the associated fame. But in the case of this particular craggy mountain in the Brecon Beacons, topped by an extensive grassy crown, it's no bad thing. For here, while cooking up a storm (either on the summit or, if the wind is too strong, on the shores of folklore-steeped Llyn y Fan Fach), the main company you will have are the red kites soaring above, or a curious badger or field vole below. Dinner guests never got so wild.

PHOEBE SMITH

# 8. ORREST HEAD, WINDERMERE, CUMBRIA, ENGLAND

It's not often that you have someone recommending walking up one of the smallest hills in England's famous fell-laden Lake District National Park – especially in a 'mountain' section of a guidebook. However, this hillock is guaranteed to give you the best views of a whole array of Lakeland peaks plus the massive expanse of Windermere – all for a mere 20 minutes' worth of walking effort. Perhaps you shouldn't overeat if opting solely for this peak. Nevertheless, it is a great vantage point to plan your adventures.

Keep an eye out for red kites and the fabled 'Lady of the Lake' ↑
when taking in the lesser known end of the Brecon Beacons

"*Tryfan is truly a monster of a mountain and one of the wonders of Snowdonia*"

Looking over to the handsome peak of Tryfan and the Glyders in Snowdonia from Pen yr Ole Wen – as mountain venues go it doesn't get much better (SS)

Indeed, it was the first peak that legendary fellwalker Alfred Wainwright climbed – the one that inspired him to walk all the others. And if it's good enough for Wainwright …

# 9. TRYFAN, GWYNEDD, WALES

Rising up above both a main road (the A5) and the sparkling waters of Llyn Ogwen, Tryfan is truly a monster of a mountain and one of the wonders of Snowdonia. Scoured by glacial action into a pointed promontory that resembles every child's drawing of a perfect peak, getting to Tryfan's top never disappoints. It's not for the faint-hearted as you need to use your hands to scramble up whichever route you take (for the uninitiated, the south side is best) and you'll need all the calories you can stomach. But when you do reach the top … let's just say that you may be eating good food, but the accompanying views you consume are truly Michelin-starred.

# 10. CROSS FELL, CUMBRIA, ENGLAND

Stretching south to north between the northern Midlands and the Tyne Gap near the borderlands of Scotland – with barely a break in the range – it's no wonder that the Pennines are known as the backbone of England. Their highest peak is not one to shout about in terms of looks, being tricky to navigate and harbouring an often-boggy plateau. But it is uniquely home to a localised phenomenon called the Helm Wind, a gust of sheer force found only on this summit. Don't worry if blowy conditions make it too hard to light the stove. Greg's Hut, a cosy bothy, sits just below the Fell's top. Consisting of two rooms, a decent-sized sleeping platform and, happily, a solid-fuel stove, it's truly an ideal place to let your inner chef run with the wind (so to speak).

# THE
# RECIPES

## CAMPER'S HACK:

MOMA (Make Oats More Awesome) do an amazing ready-mixed porridge which already has milk powder in it, in case you are in a rush ...

## ·BREAKFAST·

### ⇌ SUPER PORRIDGE ⇌

*Every porridge is super – any hiker can tell you that – but add some grains and fruit and you'll be able to keep on trekking all day long.*

## INGREDIENTS

50g porridge oats

Handful of mixed roasted seeds, eg: chia, quinoa, flax and sunflower

2 tbsp milk powder

1 sachet of sugar

Berry jam or foraged bilberries, to serve

## HERE'S THE PLAN ...

1. Turn on the camping stove, place the oats, seeds (reserving a sprinkling, to serve), milk powder and 500ml water in a pan. Cook over a medium heat for approximately 10 minutes, stirring regularly.

2. As soon as the porridge starts to bubble turn down the heat and add the sugar. Stir for another minute then remove from the heat.

3. Serve with the jam or berries and sprinkle over the reserved seeds.

## ·BREAKFAST·

### ⇒ SAUSAGE & EGG BOATS ⇐

*Feel ready to tackle even the highest mountain, with this hearty – slightly naughty – dawn delight.*

## INGREDIENTS

½ baguette or 1 small baguette

Knob of butter

1 shallot or small onion, sliced

2 meat or veggie hotdog sausages, sliced

2 eggs

Black pepper

Handful of grated Cheddar cheese

## HERE'S THE PLAN ...

1. Take the baguette and cut a V-shaped hole in the centre and gouge out the middle (you are welcome to eat this!), leaving the base intact.

2. Turn on the camping stove, melt the butter in a frying pan and add the shallot or onion and fry until softened. Add the hot dogs and cook for 5 minutes or until hot. Transfer the contents of the pan to a plate.

3. Crack the eggs into the pan and whisk through, scrambling them over a medium heat. As they start to solidify return the sliced hot dogs and shallot or onion back to the pan. Stir and season with black pepper.

4. Cook for another minute, then spoon the mixture into the hole in the bread and serve with the grated cheese sprinkled liberally on top.

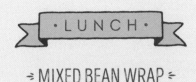

## ·LUNCH·

### ⇒ MIXED BEAN WRAP ⇐

*Healthy but filling, these quick-to-rustle-up wraps
should be in every walker's midday arsenal.*

## INGREDIENTS

½ x 400g can of mixed beans, drained

1 small avocado, peeled, stoned and sliced

Pinch of ground cumin

1 tortilla (I like beetroot tortillas here)

## HERE'S THE PLAN ...

1. Empty the beans into a bowl. Add the avocado and cumin and stir, to combine.

2. Spoon the bean mix on to the tortilla, wrap and cut in half and that's it – ready to eat!

---

## CAMPER'S HACK:

Canned tuna (use MSC-certified to be sure it is
dolphin friendly) can be added for those after an
omega-3 and protein boost.

## ⤜ WILD MUSHROOM SOUP ⤛

*Light but flavourful, and the chance to add your own
foraged mushrooms, make this a simple dish for the hills.*

## INGREDIENTS

Knob of butter

3 shallots, sliced

Handful of bought or foraged wild
   mushrooms, sliced (see box, page 29)

Handful of chestnut mushrooms, sliced

1 vegetable stock cubes

20g dried potato flakes

## HERE'S THE PLAN...

1. Turn on the camping stove and melt the butter in a saucepan until it starts to bubble. Add the shallots and fry until they start to brown.

2. Add the mushrooms and fry until they begin to soften.

3. Pour in 250ml water and crumble in the vegetable stock cube over a medium-high heat and stir well.

4. Stir in the potato flakes, bring to the boil, simmer for a couple of minutes, then serve.

# ·DINNER·

## ⇒ CHICKPEA & KALE ONE-POT STEW ⇐

*Bursting with flavour and packed with protein,*
*this single-stove stew proves that a dish with kale is*
*more than just a temporary fad.*

## INGREDIENTS

1 tbsp olive oil

Pinch ground cumin

Pinch paprika

Pinch of cinnamon

1 small onion, chopped

2 garlic cloves, chopped

50g canned chickpeas

50g curly kale, stalks removed

2 tomatoes, chopped

100g passata

## HERE'S THE PLAN ...

1. Turn on the camping stove, heat the oil in a pan until it bubbles. Add the spices and sizzle for a few seconds, stirring, then add the onion, cover and cook until the onion starts to brown, stirring occasionally.

2. Add the garlic and stir. Reduce the heat and cook for a couple of minutes then add the chickpeas and kale.

3. Stir until the kale begins to wilt and then add the tomatoes. Heat for 2 minutes, then pour in the passata. Leave to simmer for as long as you can (at least 10 minutes) and then serve.

## = DIRTY MAC, CHEESE & ONION =

*Lashings of cheese, fried onion and bacon bits make this carb-loading number a mountain-lover's go-to recipe ...*

## INGREDIENTS

100g spirali pasta (easier to eat with a spork than macaroni)

Knob of butter

1 small onion, chopped

200ml milk (you can mix 2½ tbsp milk powder and 200ml water if needed)

Handful of Cheddar cheese, grated

20g Parmesan cheese, grated

30g mozzarella, cubed

Handful of crispy bacon bits (or use crushed Frisps in an emergency!)

Black pepper

## HERE'S THE PLAN ...

1. Turn on the camping stove, bring a pan of water to the boil and cook the pasta according to the pack instructions. Drain and set aside in a bowl.

2. Melt the butter in the pan and add the onion. Fry until it browns then return the pasta to the pan. Stir together well, then pour in the milk, most of the Cheddar and all of the Parmesan and mozzarella, keep stirring to heat the mixture and to melt the cheese.

3. Once the cheese begins to melt, remove from the heat and serve. Sprinkle over the reserved Cheddar and the bacon bits and season with black pepper.

**CAMPER'S HACK:**

Quantities for this recipe should be enough
to share, making it a perfect choice
for a bothy stay...

## ·SNACKS·

# ⇒ WHISKY CHEESE FONDUE ⇐

*Forget simply sharing whisky in a
mountain hut – make more friends and indulge
with a sumptuous evening snack.*

## INGREDIENTS

1 wheel of Camembert or Brie

1 miniature bottle of whisky

Bread, bought or homemade bannock
(page 94)

**Plus** Foil

## HERE'S THE PLAN ...

1. Unwrap the cheese and pierce the top several times with a knife. Place it on a piece of foil
   and pour the whisky over the top, making sure it goes into the holes.

2. Wrap the cheese completely in the foil and place in the still-hot embers of a campfire or
   bothy stove (make sure there are no flames present).

3. Turn the wheel several times to cook it evenly until the cheese inside has melted, this should
   take around 10 minutes.

4. Remove from the embers and open the foil carefully – the cheese will be VERY hot. Dip the
   chunks of bread into the cheese to serve.

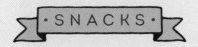

# ⇒ PHILLY & BERRY OATCAKES ⇐

*A simple idea to pimp the hill-walkers'
classic mountain staple*

## INGREDIENTS

1 small pack of oatcakes

⅓ x can berries or cherries, or a couple of
   handfuls of foraged bilberries

2 snackpacks of Philadelphia cream cheese

## HERE'S THE PLAN ...

1. Smother the oatcakes with a thick layer of cream cheese.
2. Top with the berries and enjoy. Warning — highly addictive!

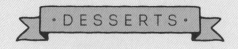

## ·DESSERTS·

### ⇒ REAL ALE PANCAKE ⇐

*Forget the milk and substitute with a good craft brew – for an indulgent and apt mountain treat.*

## INGREDIENTS

60g plain flour

2 tbsp caster sugar

½ tsp of baking powder

Pinch of salt

1 egg

125ml real ale (preferably local to the
    mountain you're on)

Knob of butter or cooking oil spray (page 17)

Whipped cream, or butter and sugar, to serve

**Plus** Spatula

## HERE'S THE PLAN ...

**1.** Place all the ingredients, except the butter or oil, into a bowl and stir well to form a smooth batter.

**2.** Turn on the camping stove and add the butter or oil to a frying pan. Heat over a high heat and once bubbling pour the batter into the pan.

**3.** Heat for a few minutes, using a spatula to loosen the mixture around the edges to ensure the pancake doesn't stick. When the mix begins to bubble, flip it and cook the other side, then flip several more times to ensure even cooking (it's all about showmanship!), then serve.

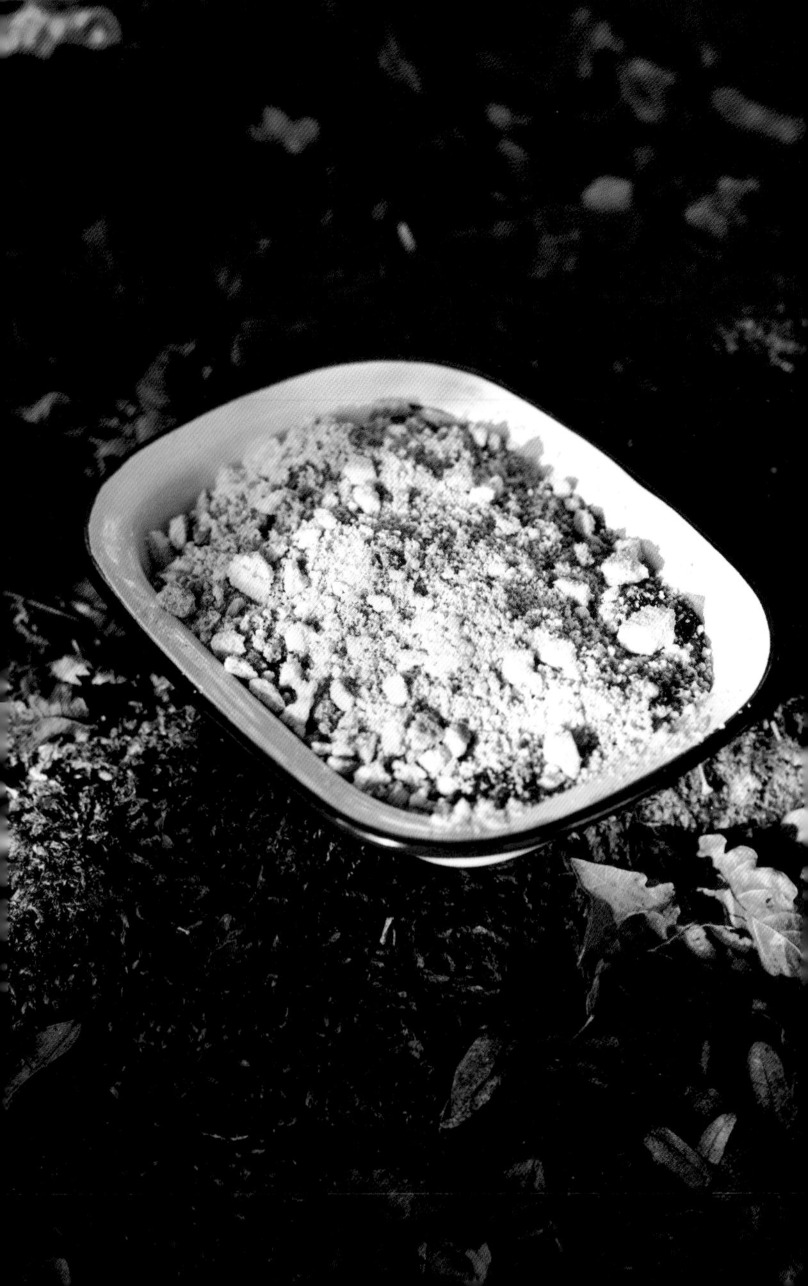

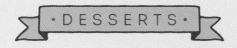

·DESSERTS·

# ⇒ COWBOY CRUMBLE ⇐

*Who says a classic can't be made quickly – pick up*
*only the very basic ingredients*
*to create an easy 'crumble' sure to fool most.*

## INGREDIENTS

½ x 400g can of mixed berries or
    cooked apples

6 Nice biscuits

## HERE'S THE PLAN ...

1. Turn on the camping stove, pour the fruit into a pan and warm over a medium heat until it starts to bubble — but don't let them boil. Pour into a bowl.

2. Crush the biscuits between your fingers over the warm fruit until it is completely covered. Serve immediately.

# RIVERSIDE

The welcoming (or maybe not so welcoming, for some) waters of the River Wharfe (JOHN POTTER/A)

'**P**ut your shoulders under – it will be fine after that!' So came the instructions when I was standing, shivering, with half my body submerged in the River Thames, near Oxford. The problem was that I didn't want to go in any further. Despite the sun's rays the water moving around my legs felt icy. Mud squelched between my toes and I swore blind that something had just touched my leg.

'Do it! Stop thinking about it and go!' My friend, a wild-swimming addict, was trying to convince me that this watery pastime was for me but – so far – was failing miserably.

Don't get me wrong – I've always loved waterways. But the thing is that I've always loved them respectfully, at a distance, from the safety of dry land. Several years ago my passion for channels became so strong that I even blew my savings on a dilapidated narrowboat. I then devoted two years of my free time to doing it up – inside and out – so that I could spend weekends and evenings on (if not in) the water.

There's something about the flow of streams, rivers and waterways that feels somehow metaphorical. It could be because I am a writer – a profession that demands creativity be turned on at the drop of a hat – working with clients who assume inspiration floats around us like the air we breathe, just waiting to be taken in and converted into intelligent words which we can spill out on to the page whenever we desire.

The reality is that writing never happens like that. Instead it is a painful teasing process that involves forcing pen to paper

*"Mud squelched between my toes and I swore blind that something had just touched my leg"*

(or, rather, fingers to keyboard) and 'making' yourself write. So imagine my surprise when, one day, while moored up in my boat by an island on my local river, I found words flowing out of me as fast as the current below. Perhaps it was fluke: maybe my muse was just being somewhere away from my desk, where distractions such as cleaning and phone calls prevent me from releasing my creative juices.

But next time I went on the water it happened again, and again. And not only when I was on the water in a boat, but even if I merely walked alongside the water, meandering on the banks without particular urgency.

And so it was that I was persuaded to try swimming in natural pools. My reasoning was that if words could come fast just by being close to a watercourse, imagine what would happen if I connected to it in a much more personal way.

Camping – and, of course, cooking – next to rivers is a dream. Not only because the scenery is pretty damn spectacular most of the time. Not merely because you can gather fish and plants to

KENNY LAM/VS

↑ A beautiful riverside camp in Glencoe

## YOUR OWN SIT MAT

Sick of getting a cold bum while slaving over your stove? Grab your knife, take some twine and get creative!

1. Look for long reeds or rushes at the water's edge. Cut yourself a fair amount — long enough to fit comfortably under your bottom when seated.

2. Gather a clump in your hand and tie them together with the middle section of a very long length of your twine, approximately 1.5m, leaving the tails of the twine to allow you to attach more sections. Do this either end of the reeds.

3. Get a second clump — the same diameter as the first — and attach this below the first one, using the tails of the twine to lash them together. Ensure that you tighten the twine securely.

4. Repeat until you have enough sections for a comfy mat. Secure the tails with a double knot. Should you wish, you can simply roll your mat and take it with you.

spruce (pardon the pun) up your meal. But also because of the sheer abundance of the essential resource that can be so difficult to find in other landscapes – water itself.

Clearly, the water you gather always needs purifying by boiling – and probably even filtering (depending where you are). But the point is that it is constantly there. What you 'harvest' can be used for drinks, for steaming, for boiling and even for cooling dishes.

The other thing that I love about rivers is that they are never isolated. They are always enshrined within another landscape. You find them within forests, snaking through mountainous scenery or high on a moorland. And this means that you get the benefit of a double helping of wild terrain.

Someone once described the waterways to me as the 'fastest way of slowing down', and that's certainly what I've found it to be. When I hike by rivers I tend to drift and amble, rather than sprint.

SEBASTIAN WASEK/A

I've followed them from source to sea – the ultimate completion of a journey. And yet rivers don't really ever have an end. They flow into bigger rivers or into estuaries or reservoirs; they are pumped into pipes or spill out into seas. But their journey is a constant one that can never truly end. And perhaps that's why I find them an infinite source of inspiration – for adventure (both physical and culinary) and for finding the right words.

Since that day when I did, eventually, find the courage to plunge not just my shoulders but also my head beneath the flowing river, I've swum in many more wild waters. Each time I still get the same sense of trepidation. On every occasion – regardless of the time of year – I always feel the chill of water against my skin. But then I also, without fail, get the same sense of refreshment, renewal and exhilaration as that first time. Perhaps this means that my relationship with Britain's waterways (and indeed all the terrains found in this country) will be never-ending too.

↑ The always-inspiring River Llugwy in Capel Curig

# FORAGE

In addition to fish – types of which will vary depending on where you are – riverside areas are also home to a couple of other handy cooking ingredients.

**WATER MINT** Water mint can be identified by its pink or bluish flowers that form clusters between July and September. To confirm, inhale the plant's minty smell, which is particularly aromatic when the leaves are crushed. Although not as sweet as other mints, water mint can be infused with hot water to make a refreshing drink. Alternatively, add it to a salad.

**REEDMACE** One of Britain's most distinctive riverside plants, reedmace has an almost cigar-like head towering above even the longest grass. It's often called cattail in the US – a nod to its appearance. In spring, the roots can be eaten raw or roasted and even ground down to make flour. Come early summer, you can use the sprouting shoots like asparagus (ie: steamed, boiled or fried). Just be sure that the plant you are harvesting is reedmace rather than the poisonous yellow flag iris, which tends to grow in similar areas but is thinner and flatter. Believe it or not, the cigar-like flower can also be eaten too – but only when young and green in the summer. Simply knock off the pollen and enjoy.

Water mint can be used as an alternative to tea ↑

# SECRET INGREDIENTS

*Water, water everywhere – but where should you head to and set up your riverside kitchen? Walk (or even paddle) this way ...*

## 1. GREAT GLEN, HIGHLANDS, SCOTLAND

Stretching from the city of Inverness in the northeast, to Ben Nevis's hometown of Fort William in the southwest, the Great Glen (which follows the Great Glen Fault) virtually tears Scotland in two. It is not strictly speaking a single river, but, more accurately, an entire 100km-worth of lochs linked by watercourses. You will be hard-pressed to find a bad spot along this waterway, but I particularly recommend the section near Laggan Locks. With an easy-to-follow path, a chance to get high in the mountains or the opportunity to stay low, it's far quieter than the tourist honeypot of nearby Loch Ness.

## 2. CLIVEDEN, BERKSHIRE, ENGLAND

Looking up from the edge of the great River Thames, just north of the Berkshire town of Maidenhead, you'll spy an intriguing estate known as Cliveden (⊘ nationaltrust.org.uk/cliveden). If you're not a National Trust member, you will need to pay to walk around the grounds of what is now a hotel. Equally pretty and entirely free, however, is the towpath that runs below. Better still, take a kayak or packraft, paddle across the Thames and set yourself up on one of the many little riverine islands, to cook a feast in Robinson Crusoe-style.

## 3. AFON GAMLAN, GWYNEDD, WALES

Tucked away deep in the landscape of North Wales – itself already home to an embarrassment of watery riches – this tumbling torrent not only provides a dramatic backdrop for a campside cookout, but has also inspired many poets and painters. Secluded between trees, Afon Gamlan boasts a collection of moss, fern and liverworts that make you feel as though you are amid a rainforest, setting the scene for you to get creative with the camping stove.

The magical Afon Gamlan ↑

## FISHING

When camping and cooking by watercourses it is understandable that adding fish to your meal might come to mind. However, do remember that there are strict laws in Britain about what you can fish and when. If using a rod, you will also need a licence (apply at ⊘ gov.uk/fishing-licences).

In English and Welsh rivers, closed season lasts from 15 March to 15 June. It is fine, however, to catch trout in still water and canals year-round. Byelaws differ in Scotland and in parts of England where additional licences may be required. Check the quirks of the waterway to which you are headed at ⊘ tinyurl.com/FishingUK.

## 4. RIVER NENE, CAMBRIDGESHIRE, ENGLAND

Meandering from Northampton city centre all the way to The Wash Estuary, the Nene is a river at its finest. For a particularly tasty section, choose the stretch between the market town of Oundle and the small green village of Fotheringhay. Wander along with your food for a waterside cooking session that's delectable in more ways than one.

## 5. DOVEDALE GORGE, PEAK DISTRICT, ENGLAND

Cutting its way through the limestone valley of the White Peak area of the Peak District National Park is the River Dove, which splits Derbyshire from Staffordshire. Surrounded by meadows filled with wild flowers, and home to many types of fish, invertebrate and water-dwelling birds such as dipper and grey heron, the best spot is found near the stepping stones beneath the shapely summit of Thorpe Cloud. Keep trekking north after you've fuelled up on food and it gets even wilder. Many think this park is all about the highs, but just add water for an even better wild night out.

NEIL S PRICE

## 6. RIVER ETIVE, GLENCOE, HIGHLAND, SCOTLAND

Running its course between the giant mountains of Glen Coe and the shores of a seawater loch 18km away is this mighty channel. Pitch a tent up along the banks of the River Etive and you'll likely be passed by scores of white-water fans attempting the myriad drops and rapids. Enjoy the spectacle as you make your food almost as spectacular as the scenery within which you're sat.

## 7. RIVER OTTER, DEVON, ENGLAND

As with other watercourses, this river is known to have inspired many a wordsmith – notably silver-tongued charmer Samuel Taylor Coleridge, who penned a sonnet to its beauty through the eyes of himself as a child. Indeed, there is something about the Otter that induces a child-like state of wonder. It could be the tunnel, known as the 'tumbling weir', where the water disappears underground. Or it might be the 'fish pass' at Otterford, where the river flows from Somerset to Devon. Or, maybe, it's the unaccounted-for presence of a new population of European

"There is something about the Otter that induces a child-like state of wonder"

The dreamy banks of the River Otter are now home to the European beaver (SS)

beaver that mysteriously appeared in 2013 along a picturesque section between Otterton and Ottery St Mary. A puzzle to ponder while preparing your food.

## 8. RIVER LLUGWY, CAPEL CURIG, CONWY, WALES

Roughly tracking the same trail as the A5 road into Snowdonia National Park, this tributary of the larger River Conwy is impressively fed by water that descends from high in the rugged Carneddau mountains. Whether dining near the torrent of Swallow Falls or heating your stew at a more sedate section near Betws-y-Coed, a meal by the Llugwy is sure to simultaneously satisfy your belly and your need for a waterside beauty spot.

## 9. RIVER WHARFE, NORTH YORKSHIRE, ENGLAND

Limestone escarpments soaring upwards, babbling pools threading through pretty villages and a 12th-century priory make the River Wharfe the perfect complement to any meal. Never too showy, unlike some of its brethren, the Wharfe allows and even encourages a mindful meander, taking in the surrounding countryside as it slowly changes from limestone to grit.

## 10. RIVER BRAAN, PERTH & KINROSS, SCOTLAND

It may not be a lengthy river, but this 17km-long tributary of the River Tay offers a waterfall so impressive that it is said – at least to me by one colourful local – that Victorian ladies couldn't even look at it without fainting. Head for the area in the gorge near Rumbling Bridge, and follow the stream to discover your perfect culinary spot where the views are knockout – but don't really knock you out (unless you are a Victorian lady, naturally).

# *THE* RECIPES

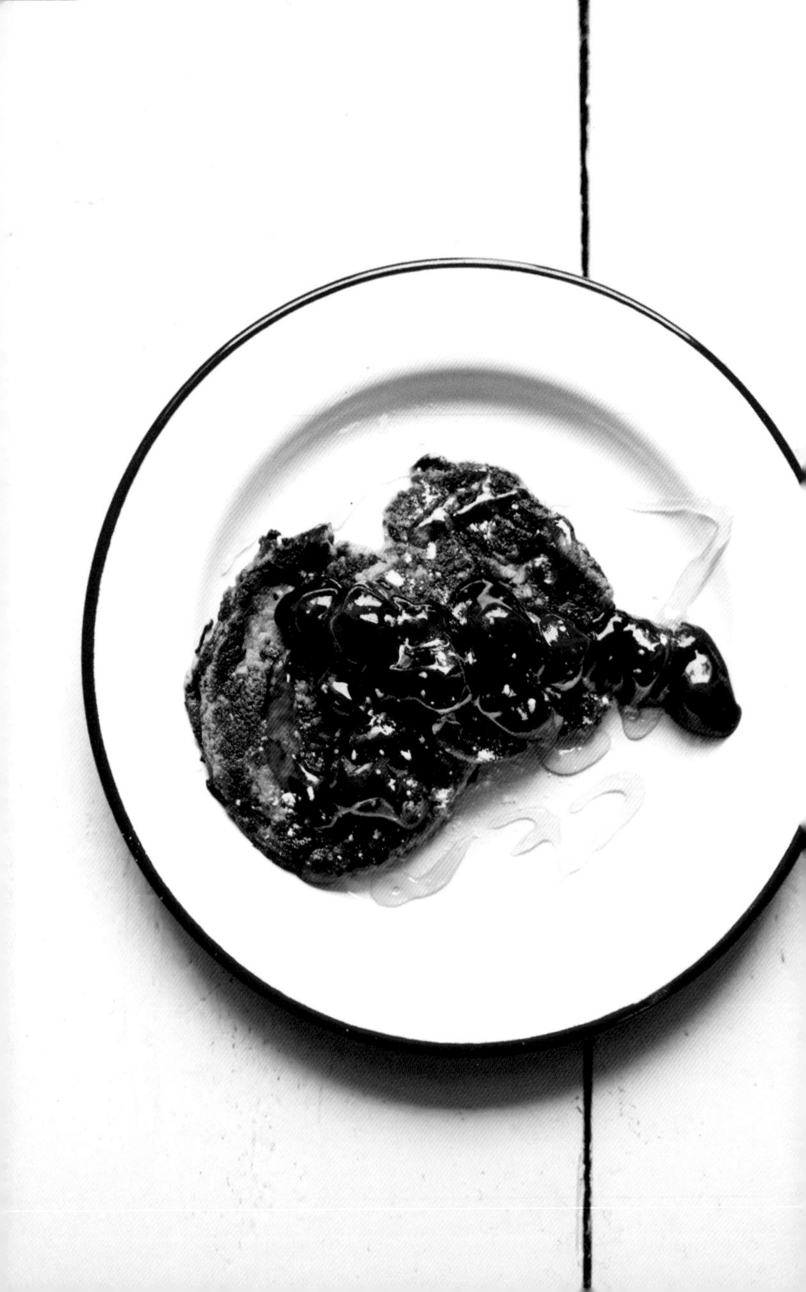

# · B R E A K F A S T ·

## ⇒ BERRY BLAST PANCAKES ⇐

*With fruit for slow-release energy and pancakes for a bit of a treat these are the pseudo-healthy way to begin a watery adventure.*

## INGREDIENTS

1 egg

250ml milk (or 250ml water mixed with
  3 tbsp powdered milk)

350g self-raising flour

Large knob of butter or splash of cooking oil

⅓ x 400g canned or fresh mixed berries

Clear honey, to serve

## HERE'S THE PLAN ...

1. Mix the egg, milk and flour together in a bowl to form a smooth batter.

2. Stir in two-thirds of the berries – the mixture will turn a lovely shade of purple.

3. Turn on the camping stove and heat some of the butter or oil in a frying pan until sizzling hot. Place two spoonfuls of the mixture into the pan, to make two pancakes. (You should be able to cook two small American-style pancakes at a time in most camping frying pans.)

4. As the batter starts to bubble, flip the pancakes, to cook on the second side.

5. Once cooked, transfer to a plate and cook a further two pancakes with the remaining batter. Serve with a scattering of berries and a drizzle of honey.

## CAMPER'S HACK:

You can, of course, buy a 'just add water'
pancake mix, which you can then simply add
the berries to and shake together.
This is worth it if there's a few of you.

# · B R E A K F A S T ·

## ⇒ EGG-STRA SPECIAL BREAD ⇒

*Add some local cheese to make a simple recipe
a whole lot more indulgent ...*

## INGREDIENTS

1 egg

Handful of grated cheese (local if possible)

Knob of butter

2 slices of bread

Sachet of tomato ketchup (optional)

## HERE'S THE PLAN ...

1. Mix the egg and cheese together in a bowl.

2. Turn on the camping stove and heat the knob of butter in a frying pan until it bubbles.

3. Dip one slice of bread in the egg mixture, turn the bread to coat the other side.

4. Place in the pan and fry for 2 minutes per side, turning occasionally. Remove from the pan.

5. Repeat for the second slice and then serve.

## ⇌ 'SUPER' NOODLES ⇌

*Forget the boring pre-packed variety; prepare your own
healthy noodles pre-trip for a perfect meal on the go.*

## INGREDIENTS

100g egg or rice noodles (rice ones cook
   quicker, but are less filling)
½ vegetable or chicken stock cube
Handful of grated carrot

½ x 140g can or 50g frozen peas
Handful of fresh mushrooms, sliced
Pinch of paprika
**Plus** Heatproof plastic food box with lid

## HERE'S THE PLAN...

### Before you go

1. Cook the noodles, following the pack instructions. Drain and then rinse in cold water. Place
   in a heatproof lidded plastic food box.

2. Crumble the stock cube over the noodles and add the paprika and cover with the carrot.

3. Add the peas and mushrooms and stir well. Seal and store in the fridge.

### In the wild

1. When you're ready to eat, simply boil a pan of water and slowly pour the water over the
   noodles, to cover. Stir well and replace the lid.

2. Wait for 5 minutes, stir again, then serve.

# ⇒ PINEAPPLE FRIED RICE ⇐

*A quick and light lunch that combines the energy of carbs with the sweetness and quick hit of fruit.*

## INGREDIENTS

Single-portion pack of boil-in-the-bag rice

1 tsp olive oil

1 small onion, sliced

1 garlic clove, crushed

½ x 230g can of pineapple chunks, drained

Pinch of ground ginger

1 tbsp soy or Worcestershire sauce

## HERE'S THE PLAN ...

1. Turn on the camping stove and cook the boil-in-the-bag, following the pack instructions. Rinse bag in cold water to prevent overcooking and set aside.

2. Heat the oil in a frying pan until it bubbles and then add the onion and cook until it softens and begins to brown.

3. Add the garlic and stir fry for another minute then throw in the pineapple and ginger. Stir fry for about 4 minutes, until everything browns.

4. Add the rice and stir, then pour over the soy or Worcestershire sauce, stir fry for 2–3 minutes. Serve straight away.

## ⇒ ONE-PAN PIZZA ⇐

*Don't worry – no woodfired oven is required to make the camper's cheat version of the delicious Italian staple.*

## INGREDIENTS

145g pack pizza base mix
2 tbsp olive oil
2 shallots, sliced
1 garlic clove, crushed
Pinch of dried basil

8 cherry tomatoes, chopped
2 tbsp passata
½ x 200g tube tomato purée
Handful of grated Cheddar

## HERE'S THE PLAN ...

1. Make up the pizza base mix following the pack instructions. Knead the mixture together to form a stretchy, non-sticky dough. Set aside.

2. Heat half the olive oil in the frying pan and add the shallots, garlic and basil and cook over a medium heat until softened. Add the halved tomatoes and passata and simmer for around 5 minutes. Once warmed through, remove from the heat and pour into a bowl.

3. Heat the remaining oil in the frying pan and place the dough into it, fitting it to the size and shape of the pan (removing excess if needed) – keep it to around 3cm thick. Keep cooking by pressing it with the back of a spork into the pan – it'll start to rise.

4. After about 7 minutes squeeze the purée on to the base and spread with the back of your spork. Spread the cooked tomato mixture on to the base and sprinkle the cheese over.

5. Continue to cook and when the cheese has melted, it's ready to serve.

# ⇌ MUSHROOM & POTATO SPICED STEW ⇌

*Treat yourself to a hearty evening dish,
with added spice for extra kick, after this you'll not
have mush-room for pudding.*

## INGREDIENTS

Knob of butter

2 shallots, finely chopped

1 baked potato, baked in advance, skin on
   and sliced thickly

Handful of small foraged or bought
   mushrooms, whole (see box, page 29)

½ vegetable stock cube

½ x 400g can coconut milk

Pinch of ground coriander

1 tbsp Tikka Masala curry paste

1 naan bread

## HERE'S THE PLAN ...

1. Turn on the camping stove and melt the butter in a pan, when bubbling, add the shallots,
   potato and mushrooms. Cook for around 5 minutes, until everything browns and softens.

2. Crumble in the vegetable stock cube and stir in the coconut milk, coriander and curry paste.

3. Reduce the heat and cook gently for 8–10 minutes, stirring occasionally. Warm naan bread
   on a plate over the stew while it is cooking.

4. Serve the curry with the naan bread.

## ⇒ HOMEMADE HUMMUS ⇐

*Yes, you can cheat and buy pre-packed,
but when it comes to hummus, homemade definitely
tastes better. Mix the spices together before you
leave home to make it really easy.*

## INGREDIENTS

Pinch of ground cumin

Pinch of turmeric powder

Pinch of paprika

Pinch of sea salt

½ x 400g can chickpeas

1 tbsp tahini

1 garlic clove, crushed

Splash of lemon juice

1 tbsp olive oil

2 pita breads

**Plus** Cooking fork

## HERE'S THE PLAN ...

1. Turn on the camping stove and boil a small pan of water. Find a medium stone (for crushing the ingredients) and pour water over it, to clean it. Place the spices, chickpeas, tahini, garlic, lemon juice and olive oil together in a bowl with 2 tbsp water.

2. Crush the ingredients together with the stone. Keep going until most of the larger lumps have been crushed – though a few whole chickpeas are fine.

3. Heat the pita breads over the camping stove flame for a few minutes to warm them.

4. To serve, simply dip the pita straight into the hummus.

·SNACKS·

# ⇒ MARSHMALLOW MADNESS ⇐

*A childhood classic that can lead to sticky fingers, but well worth it for a delightful campside treat.*

## INGREDIENTS

10g butter
75g marshmallows

50g puffed rice breakfast cereal
**Plus** Non-stick silicone paper

## HERE'S THE PLAN ...

1. Line a mess tin with non-stick silicone paper. Turn the camping stove on, and slowly melt the butter in a pan.
2. Add the marshmallows to the pan and continue to heat, stirring often, until the marshmallows melt to form a sticky liquid.
3. Remove the pan from the stove and add the puffed rice and mix the ingredients together quickly, before they harden.
4. Spoon the mixture into the lined tin and press it down with the back of a spork.
5. Leave to cool for about 30 minutes, then break off pieces and enjoy.

## · DESSERTS ·

### ⇌ NICE 'N' NUTTY ⇌

*Make use of fast-flowing, cooling water to make this energy-laden treat that will keep for days.*

## INGREDIENTS

200g granulated sugar
Pinch of sea salt
100g mix of salted peanuts and cashews

Spray cooking oil (page 17)
**Plus** Non-stick silicone baking paper

## HERE'S THE PLAN ...

1. Mix together the sugar, salt and 120ml water.

2. Turn on the camping stove and heat the oil in a frying pan. Pour the sugar mix into the pan and heat, without stirring.

3. When the sugar starts to turn golden, start stirring the mix occasionally until all the sugar has melted and there's a golden liquid left, this will take around 8–10 minutes. While you're waiting, line a mess tin with non-stick silicone baking paper.

4. Take the pan off the heat and stir the nuts into the liquid.

5. Pour the mixture into the lined tin and spread it around evenly; it should be no more than 2cm deep.

6. Set aside to cool, to do this take advantage of the river and dip the base (only don't get the contents wet!) into the water, to cool it faster. It will harden into a tasty brittle after about 15–20 minutes. To eat, simply break into pieces.

## ⇌ BAKED APPLE & GINGER BOMBS ⇌

*Let the flavour explode on your taste buds with
this fruity after-dinner delight.*

## INGREDIENTS

1 eating apple (I like pink or red best)
50g granola
Pinch of ground cinnamon

Pinch of ground ginger
**Plus** Foil

## HERE'S THE PLAN ...

1. Partially core the apple, leaving the base in place. Chop the top 1cm off the removed core and set aside to keep as a plug. Discard the remaining core.
2. Mix the granola in a bowl with the cinnamon and ginger then pour the mixture into the hole in the apple and replace with the top.
3. Wrap the apple in foil and place in the embers of a campfire or Kelly Kettle for 15–20 minutes or until tender.
4. Remove from the fire and enjoy. Beware – contents will be very hot!

# WOODLAND

The Forest of Dean — home to some of the best dens around (SS)

I was being followed. The unmistakable sounds of branches cracking and leaves rustling were growing ever closer. Here in a pocket of wild woodland, close to my home, I stopped and decided to hide from my pursuer. A huge fallen oak tree provided an ideal place. Coated with a layer of green moss that dangled from the oak's trunk as though an alien form of old spiderwebs, the tree was almost inviting me to seek solace amid its myriad branches. I lay down behind it, among the vibrant foxgloves and yellow pimpernel, and covered myself with leaves, breathing slowly and as quietly as I could.

Despite Hollywood movies and childhood stories telling us that the woods are full of danger, there was nothing sinister about this scene. Instead, it was merely a typical day in my childhood, when my neighbour and I would play hide-and-seek in the forest. In reality, there was no murderer on my trail, no fierce creature hunting me down. There was nothing but me and native trees – beech, chestnut and spindly firs – stretching up into the sky.

Yet somewhere between the innocence of youth – making dens in hollowed-out trunks and climbing trees – and becoming a proper adult, our excitement at spending time in these magical places morphs into an unnatural fear of the forest. For many, the foreboding nature of clusters of trees is scary. Enter a woodland and the temperature drops – causing you to shiver (although, in summer, this may count as welcome shade). Sit still for just a minute and you will, undoubtedly, hear the movement of some invisible creature in the undergrowth (for wildlife lovers this is part of the thrill). Lose your way, and the lack of distinguishable landmarks can cause you to become disorientated very, very quickly (though, for adventurers, this is how you learn to navigate).

*"The tree was almost inviting me to seek solace amid its myriad branches"*

PHOEBE SMITH

But when it comes to forests, fear is misplaced because Britain's roots can be found in the trees. In fact – had it not been for humankind, most of our fair island (and isles) would be covered in a mix of broadleaf trees – with English oak being the dominant species. With forests cleared to make way for farming, and obliterated by the need for timber to build ships and planes in wars throughout history, the UK's woodland has been depleted to now account for just 12% of our terrain.

As such, I believe that it is vital that trees should be celebrated. They give us so much – from wood for our fires and building materials, to homes for an abundance of wildlife and they even emit the oxygen that we breathe. They offer a place for both exploration and veneration of the ancient (some trees are hundreds if not thousands of years old). So woodlands are not to be feared, but rather appreciated like a wise, knowing relative. For trees have seen it all before. As they have grown – slowly, steadily over centuries – they have witnessed abundant change. Many will outlive all of us, providing a constant across the generations.

When I began to renew my love of the forest – after years as a young adult dreading what lay behind the dark trees – I met a ranger in Ennerdale, a forested landscape in the Lake District

↑ Wandering through the moss-covered branches on the North Dorset coastline

# HOW TO MAKE STINGING NETTLES SAFE TO EAT

**TOP TIP**

Tasting a bit like mild spinach, nettles are not only a great accompaniment to a meal, they are also good for you. As well as being packed full of protein, iron and vitamins, herbalists use them to treat allergies and arthritis. But how do you make these stingers 'safe'? No problem – provided you follow these simple steps:

1. First, collect the right leaves in the right way. Wearing gloves, look for younger green leaves (near the top of the plant) with no white spittle on the underside. Remove a handful by cutting them from the stems (you only want the leaves themselves).

2. To clean the nettle leaves, submerge them in hot (not boiling) water for 15 minutes. At this point you can remove your gloves. Once done, drain the water and start boiling some more fresh water.

3. Add a pinch of salt to it, and add the leaves, stirring for 5 minutes. Any sting will subside in around 30 seconds so do not worry about handling the leaves without gloves).

4. Remove the leaves from the boiling water and plunge straight into a bowl of the coldest water you can get. Remove from the cold water after a few seconds and dry on a towel/clothing.

5. The leaves are now ready – you can fry them, add them to soup or simply chop them and add as a garnish.

"Woodlands are not to be feared,
but rather appreciated like a wise,
knowing relative"

Wild Wistman's Wood in Dartmoor (55)

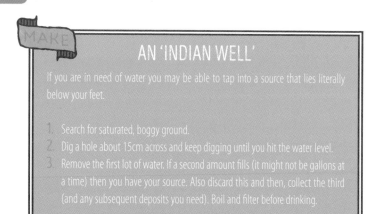

MAKE

## AN 'INDIAN WELL'

If you are in need of water you may be able to tap into a source that lies literally below your feet.

1.   Search for saturated, boggy ground.
2.   Dig a hole about 15cm across and keep digging until you hit the water level.
3.   Remove the first lot of water. If a second amount fills (it might not be gallons at a time) then you have your source. Also discard this and then, collect the third (and any subsequent deposits you need). Boil and filter before drinking.

that is gradually being allowed to rewild. He was telling me about the plans for the area, about the planting of slow-growing native broadleaf trees that will eventually replace the introduced fast-sprouting conifers. He led me up a fellside and explained what it would one day look like.

'But you'll never live to see it,' I said, and with a growing realisation added: 'And neither will I.' He simply smiled and answered: 'That's the work of a forest caretaker. We plant for the benefit of the future, not for the instant gratification of today.' Knowing that the forest where we stood was planted as an emergency measure to help the enormous demand for timber during World War I, his assertion felt utterly fitting.

Since that day I have begun to explore more woodland to appreciate its place in our world and to enjoy it during the small segment of time I will get to experience it. If there's a plaque I look at who planted the trees, wanting to know more about the soul who first sowed the sapling seed, fully aware that they would never see it mature.

On such explorations, I always take my hammock to string between two trees. I allow myself time to sway to sleep or even

> *"I find woodland to be one of the most inspiring landscapes in which to prepare a meal"*

just to sit, rest and soak it all in. Sometimes, though, I don't even use the hammock, instead I build my own lean-to shelter or find a hollowed tree inside which to climb and truly feel part of the forest.

As for wild cooking, I find woodland to be one of the most inspiring landscapes in which to prepare a meal. Not only do forests offer handy 'shelves' on tree stumps and natural hooks (branches) from which to dangle bags, they also offer a huge array of foraging opportunities, especially when autumn comes and fungi fruit. Woodlands are always giving, never asking.

Although I no longer enter woodlands to hide from a friend while playing a childhood game, I do still seek solace within them. Even just for a few hours, they enable me to disappear from a world obsessed with looking to the future, and in some way grant me access to our ancestors, allowing me to pass through the areas where those we will never meet gave up an easy life to toil through their tomorrows, to give us shade in our today.

PHOEBE SMITH

A quickly made lean-to shelter can make you feel truly at one with the woodland ↑

## TOP TIP

# HOW TO BUILD A CAMPFIRE

There's nothing as cosy as sitting in front of a blazing campfire, but before you even take match to tinder, you need to know that you're allowed to do it. Always check first, as you don't want to risk damaging an ecosystem or burning down an entire forest. Assuming you are in an area where fires are permitted, follow these steps to get the fire going:

1. Gather tinder (dry leaves, bark or fungi): these are the things that catch fire quickly and burn fast. They will form the centre of your fire.
2. Collect kindling (dry, thin branches and sticks). Form items into a small tipi structure around the tinder pile. They will be ignited by the fast-burning tinder but burn slower.
3. Find the fuel (large logs and branches). These will burn the slowest and give out the most heat. Avoid gathering items that are so big that they won't catch fire. These should also be placed, tipi-like, around the kindling.
4. Light the tinder by placing a match on it so it catches fire. Once alight it will burn the kindling, which will then burn the fuel. As the fire gets going the tipis will collapse. This is fine; simply add more fuel once it is burning well.
5. Get out the guitar — sorry, I mean marshmallows, of course . . .

PHOEBE SMITH

# SECRET INGREDIENTS

*Knowing what to cook to complement your tree-lined surrounds is one thing, but where should you hang your hammock and get cooking? Here's a cluster of wild woodlands for you to sample.*

## 1. THIRLMERE FOREST, CUMBRIA, ENGLAND

The Lake District National Park in Cumbria may be best known for its hills, but it's also home to some rather special woodland. Look on a map at the west side of Thirlmere Reservoir and you can't help but notice the length of green spread along its banks and rising towards the little-visited peaks of High Seat and Bleaberry Fell. The forest here is perfect foraging territory for fungi come autumn, not to mention home to trees that can take a hammock.

## 2. BRADLEY WOODS, LINCOLNSHIRE, ENGLAND

They often say it's grim up north, but seeking to disprove this statement is the 32km-long path known as the Wanderlust Way. Taking in a range of villages, farmland and limestone cliffs, it starts in a quaint little copse of trees called Bradley Woods. Walk the trail first to really build up an appetite, but don't be tempted by

Known for fells and lakes, Cumbria's Lake District National Park
is also home to wonderful woodland (ROBERT READ/A)

the pub in the last village before you finish. Instead settle in for a forest feast (the handy thing being that your car can be parked nearby so you can take extra food and be even more adventurous with your cooking). It's certainly an atmospheric spot and one that has spawned folklore about a mysterious 'black lady' who is said to be on an endless search for her baby who was snatched during the 15th-century War of the Roses. Now there's something to contemplate while you enjoy your hot chocolate …

## 3. KINGLEY VALE, WEST SUSSEX, ENGLAND

A visit to this nature reserve in the South Downs on the doorstep of Chichester is, for many, akin to stopping by to see the relatives. That's because the yew trees that you'll find in the woodland are among some of the oldest living things in Britain (2,000 years young). Amid the fallen leaves and knotted tree trunks are not one but 14 scheduled ancient monuments. This means that you can cook and eat, then indulge your inner Indiana Jones by hunting for remains of ancient civilisations. Say it with me: 'It belongs in a museum!'.

## 4. OXSHOTT HEATH, SURREY, ENGLAND

It is important to note that little patches of wild woodland occur all over the British Isles – even close to major cities. Just 20 miles from London, the woodland in Oxshott is a case in point. Featuring silver birch, Scots pine and oak trees, it has a network of meandering paths that lead to an open common which reputedly served as a baseball pitch for Canadian troops stationed here during both world wars. Look out for remains of the sand pit – incidentally, a good spot to set up your 'kitchen' – which was created in the late 19th century for building, then used during World War II to fill sandbags.

# FORAGE

There is nothing quite so terrifying to a newbie forager than the idea of picking mushrooms, but British woodlands are abundant with species ripe for the picking. Just remember the rules:

- If in any doubt, don't eat it: it's never worth the risk (for more information, see box page 29).
- Get a good field guide (page 221) and take it with you. There are more than 15,000 species in Britain alone so start by picking a handful of edible species to learn thoroughly.
- Avoid 'shrooms with white gills (on the underside of the cap) and any that grow in a cup (aka volva).
- Cooking them is better than eating raw (and always wash thoroughly).

As well as fungi, keep an eye out for beechnuts. These are found in kernels beneath beech trees. For a perfect snack on the move, peel the arrow-shaped shells and eat the fleshy nut inside.

The edible parasol mushroom, *Lepiota procera*, is a good species for novice foragers ↑

JAMES LOWEN

## 5. BEDLAM WOOD, KENT, ENGLAND

If one woodland was chosen to be on this list for name alone, then this hillside patch in the Kent Downs would unequivocally be it. Situated near the comely village of Lyminge, Bedlam is accessed via the Elham Valley Way which forms part of a new pilgrimage route – The Old Way – devised by the British Pilgrim Trust in 2017. Bedlam Wood may be small but it boasts carpets of bluebells in spring plus gnarled, twisted branches through which you can squeeze – although this is perhaps best done before you've eaten your hearty fare.

## 6. ENNERDALE FOREST, CUMBRIA, ENGLAND

If ever there was a poster child for 'rewilding' then the Lake District's Ennerdale is undoubtedly it. Once uniformly controlled by man, since a joint initiative was started by the landowners ten years ago, the whole woodland has been allowed to break free of its linear shackles, growing higgledy-piggledy, while the River Liza that cuts through Ennerdale has been permitted to change its course. Rangers here encourage exploration, making it the ideal place to pack your hammock, stove and food – and then get creative in both culinary hiking and aspirations.

↑ European kestrels can be spotted hovering above Silent Valley in Gwent

## 7. SILENT VALLEY, EBBW VALE, WALES

Silent Valley is nestled in Gwent's heartland. To look at this lush band of beech, alder and hawthorn trees now, you would never guess that this place was once a coal pit. In fact, many of the mounds you see today – coated in a handy picnic blanket-like collection of heather, grass and soft moss – were formed when shale was dumped from digs back in the mining boom of the 18th and 19th centuries. Further down the valley reclaimed landfill has been taken over by nature with woodpeckers, cuckoos and kestrels now frequent visitors, while the very path along which you walk was a track cleaved by horses pulling out the miner's spoils on carts. This is truly a landscape of hidden depths: just ensure your belly is equally as deep when you prepare your meal.

## 8. COED-Y-FELIN, FLINTSHIRE, NORTH WALES

In a list full of big hitters (in terms of long-standing woodland), with histories that span hundreds more years than they are metres tall, it seems only fair to nod to a much younger forest. Just outside the rather unfortunately named Welsh village of Mold, is the ten-year-old offering of Coed-y-Felin. Designed and planted by the local community it has a mix of native broadleaf trees, within easy reach of walking trails at the well-established hill of Moel Famau and its adjacent country park, Coed-y-Felin. The wood offers uplifting proof of what wonderful things can happen when small communities come together. An idea that's definitely easy to stomach.

## 9. AMAT FOREST, HIGHLAND, SCOTLAND

Set in the northernmost reaches of mainland Britain, over an hour's drive even from the self-proclaimed 'Gateway to the Highlands'

NATURE PICTURE LIBRARY/A

of Inverness, is this mammoth collection of pine trees. Having existed in this far-flung Scottish region for centuries, legend has it that the Vikings used timber from Amat to build their great ships, floating trunks down the nearby River Carron to the sea. Amat Forest is situated on the Alladale Estate, whose name may ring bells – for it is here that there has been serious and controversial talk (or should that be howls?) of reintroducing wolves.

## 10. TAYNISH, ARGYLL, SCOTLAND

Flung out on a westerly peninsula, overlooking the Inner Hebridean isle of Jura, Taynish comprises a collection of ancient woods that themselves harbour some of the oldest examples of oaks found in Britain. Interspersed between those old wizened trunks are examples of alder, ash and birch, which of themselves provide homes to otters, pipistrelle bats and red squirrels; and rare marsh fritillary butterflies flit in more open areas of the reserve. Taynish is also close to Loch Coille Bharr, which is home to a recent reintroduction of the once-extinct European beaver – meaning you can now have good food with a mini-safari on the side.

↑ Wild woodland and wild river in Taynish, the perfect pairing

# THE RECIPES

## ·BREAKFAST·

### ⇒ DEVILED EGGS IN DISGUISE ⇐

*A Moroccan slant on the usual boiled egg and soldiers,
packed with earthy spices to seamlessly
blend with your forest surrounds.*

## INGREDIENTS

2 eggs
2 pita breads
Pinch of paprika

Pinch of ground cumin
Pinch of all-season spice
Pinch of turmeric

## HERE'S THE PLAN ...

1. Turn on the camping stove and bring a pan of water to the boil. Add the eggs and boil for 6 minutes. Drain the eggs and plunge into cold water to cool.

2. Once the eggs are cool, peel and slice.

3. Heat the pita over the flame of the stove for a few minutes, then split open with a knife.

4. Sprinkle the spices over the egg slices, pop inside the warmed pita and enjoy.

## CAMPER'S HACK:

Measure the spices into a single small
container before you go to save some weight
in the backpack. You may want to
take a little ketchup too!

## CAMPER'S HACK:

This recipe will make more bannock bread
than you can eat in one go, but it keeps well,
simply wrap it in foil or in a
plastic food box and enjoy later.

## ·BREAKFAST·

### ⇒ RAISIN BREAD ⇐

*Bannock bread with a breakfast twist,
the perfect way to wake up in the woods.*

## INGREDIENTS

400g self-raising flour

Handful of raisins

7 tbsp powdered milk

2 tsp baking powder

Pinch of salt

Knob of butter

Clear honey, to serve

**Plus** Foil or plastic food box with lid

## HERE'S THE PLAN...

1. Place all the ingredients, apart from the butter and honey, in a bowl and mix together.

2. Gradually add enough cold water, mixing with your hands, to form a slightly sticky dough.

3. Knead the dough until the raisins are evenly spread throughout it.

4. Grease a frying pan or mess tin with half the butter and then press the bread into it, shaping it to fit the container.

5. Heat the pan or tin slowly on the stove, continuously moving the bread and turning it over as it begins to crisp so that it doesn't stick.

6. The bread will rise as it heats and will be ready in about 10 minutes. Once browned and hollow-sounding when tapped, serve with the remaining butter and a dollop of honey.

# CAMPER'S HACK:

If available, to save time, you can always
buy a pre-seasoned couscous mix -
recommended substitute is
Ainsley Harriott's Moroccan Medley!

## ⇒ CRACKING COUSCOUS ⇐

*The old adage says 'it's so nice they named it twice' –
clearly that person had tried
this version of the deliciously simple dish.*

## INGREDIENTS

100g couscous
100ml boiling water
1 small pomegranate
Pinch of ground coriander

Pinch of ground cinnamon
Pinch of dried mint
Pinch of salt

## HERE'S THE PLAN ...

1. Put the couscous in a bowl and cover with the boiling water, stirring well. Cover (perhaps use your Buff or hat) and leave for around 6 minutes.

2. While waiting, halve the pomegranate.

3. Once the couscous has absorbed all the water, scoop the pomegranate seeds into the bowl. Add the spices, mint and salt and stir until it's well mixed, then serve warm.

## ·LUNCH·

### ⇒ BRILLIANT BURRITOS ⇒

*Spice up your life with a warming
Mexican-style wrap – perfect for chilly days
when heather bashing in the forest.*

## INGREDIENTS

½ x 400g can of refried beans

Pinch of paprika

Pinch of ground cumin

1 small avocado, peeled, stoned and sliced

Handful of grated cheese (I prefer Mexicana)

2 tortillas

Cooking oil spray (page 17)

## HERE'S THE PLAN ...

1. Turn on the camping stove and place the refried beans in a pan, warm over a medium heat for 5–7 minutes until bubbling but not boiling. Add the spices and heat for another 2 minutes, stirring regularly.

2. Place the avocado and half the cheese in the centre of the tortilla. Top with the beans and remaining cheese, then roll the tortilla.

3. Spray the frying pan with a little oil and add the filled tortilla, pressing it down slightly, and cook for a couple of minutes on each side to heat through.

4. Tuck in – but remember contents will be HOT!

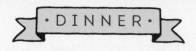

## ⇒ MOLTEN CHEESE JACKET ⇐

*Feel every bit the fancy chef, by not only cooking your spud to perfection on your campfire, but by finishing it off nicely with a burned blast of cheese.*

## INGREDIENTS

2 small baking potatoes (pre-microwaved for 8 minutes if possible)

Handful of grated Red Leicester cheese

**Plus** Foil, blowtorch lighter

## HERE'S THE PLAN ...

1. Wrap the potatoes in foil and chuck on to a campfire, turning occasionally. The longer you leave them the better — around 30 minutes if microwaved or up to 1 hour if not.

2. Check to see if the potatoes are ready by how easily a spork penetrates the inside. When they are cooked cut a cross in the top of both spuds.

3. Sprinkle the cheese on top of the potatoes. Using a blowtorch lighter, melt the cheese. Alternatively, simply rewrap the potatoes and throw back in the fire for an additional 10 minutes. Serve.

CAMPER'S HACK:
Make this a fuller meal and serve with
Cracking Couscous (page 204).

## ⇌ ROSEMARY & GARLIC MUSHROOMS ⇌

*Whether foraging for your own fungi or picking some up in the shops en route, this quick dish will leave you without much-room for seconds!*

## INGREDIENTS

Splash of olive oil
1 small shallot, thinly sliced
2 garlic cloves, thinly sliced
Sprig of fresh rosemary

5 Portobello mushrooms or a selection of
    foraged mushrooms (see box, page 29)
Splash of red wine

## HERE'S THE PLAN ...

1. If possible, cook over a wood-fuelled Kelly Kettle to enhance the smoky flavour.

2. Turn on the camping stove and heat the olive oil in a frying pan until it bubbles then add the shallot, garlic and rosemary and stir continuously until softened.

3. Add the mushrooms and stir to coat with the oil.

4. Sizzle for a couple of minutes, then add the wine, reduce the heat and cook for a further 3 minutes. Serve.

## ·SNACKS·

## ⇒ ANTS ON LOGS ⇐

*You may have heard of their celery cousins,*
*but opt for apple instead for a sweet,*
*juicy treat between meals.*

### INGREDIENTS

1 eating apple (I like Granny Smith)

6 tbsp crunchy peanut butter

Handful of raisins

### HERE'S THE PLAN ...

1. Cut the apple into equal portions and cut out the core and pips.

2. Top with a good dollop of peanut butter and decorate with a cluster of raisins. Enjoy the sweet and savoury goodness!

# ·SNACKS·

## ⇒ CAMPER'S FOREST FRITTATA ⇐

*Fill your boots – and belly – with this energy-inducing
Spanish favourite, with added woodland fungi.*

## INGREDIENTS

Cooking oil spray (page 17)
1 small onion, sliced
1 small courgette, sliced
6 cherry tomatoes, halved

Handful of foraged mushrooms (see box,
        page 29), sliced
4 eggs
Pinch of sea salt
Handful of grated Cheddar cheese

## HERE'S THE PLAN ...

1. Turn on the camping stove, spray a frying pan with some oil and heat it over a high heat.
   Once the oil starts to bubble, add all the vegetables and cook for about 5 minutes until
   tender, stirring frequently.

2. Mix the eggs and salt in a bowl and pour evenly over the vegetables in the pan, making sure
   everything is covered. Sprinkle the cheese over the top.

3. Reduce the heat and use a plate to cover the pan to ensure more even cooking. Turn the
   frittata occasionally by sliding it on to a plate and then turning it back into the pan.

4. When the middle has set, after around 8–10 minutes, serve.

## = BBQ BANANAS =

*Pack a protein punch and satiate your sugar craving
with this sumptuous banana-based offering.*

## INGREDIENTS

1 or 2 bananas (the riper the better)
Handful of mini-marshmallows
Handful of milk chocolate chips
Sprinkling of peanuts or almonds

Whipped cream in a can (optional
    luxury treat)
**Plus** Foil

## HERE'S THE PLAN ...

1. Slice the unpeeled bananas, through the skin, along one side and stuff the middle with half
   the mini-marshmallows and all the chocolate chips.
2. Wrap in foil and place in the embers of a Kelly Kettle.
3. After around 6 minutes the contents will have melted. Remove and serve with yet more
   marshmallows, a sprinkling of peanuts and a squirt of cream, if you like, for a banana-split
   sundae — camper's style!

**CAMPER'S HACK:**

Some cake mixes only need you to add water - which will save you time and the need to carry an egg.

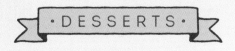

## ·DESSERTS·

### ⇒ CHOCOLATE ORANGES ⇐

*Fun for adults and kids alike – these fire-cooked
chocolate cakes combine with vitamin-C rich fruit for
a treat you only have to feel half guilty about.*

## INGREDIENTS

½ x 400g pack chocolate sponge cake mix

1 egg

3 oranges (navel are best)

**Plus** Foil

## HERE'S THE PLAN ...

1. Place the cake mix in a bowl, add the egg and 60ml water. Mix all the ingredients together, until smooth. Set aside.

2. Cut the top of each orange and reserve the tops for later. Hollow out the flesh of the oranges, removing any rind, pith and seeds, and add the flesh to the chocolate cake mix and stir well.

3. Pour the mixture into each of the orange shells, they should be about three-quarters full.

4. Replace the lids and wrap each orange in foil and place on to the Kelly Kettle fire.

5. The mix normally takes 10–15 minutes to rise. Check after 10 minutes by sticking your spork into the cake; if the mix is done then it will come out clean. When ready, serve to enjoy your very own chocolate orange.

# FURTHER INFO
## AND
# USEFUL RESOURCES

## WEBSITES

⌀ **basecampfood.com** Offers perhaps the widest range of pre-made camping food in the UK.

⌀ **darksky.org** International Dark Sky Association, with useful details on their accredited reserves, places, communities and sanctuaries.

⌀ **www.dartmoor.gov.uk/about-us/about-us-maps/new-camping-map** A fantastically detailed interactive map of Dartmoor National Park on suggested wild camp spots.

⌀ **forestry.gov.uk** Detailed information on the Forestry Commission's woodlands in England, Wales and Scotland.

⌀ **www.gov.uk/fishing-licences** For up-to-date information about where you can and can't fish in the UK and application forms for fishing licences (one-day, eight-day or 12-month available).

⌀ **jetboil.com** The author's favoured easy-to-use camping stoves.

⌀ **www.kellykettle.com** The best way to have a 'safe' campfire that won't leave any nasty scorch marks on the ground.

⌀ **ldwa.org.uk** Official site for the Long-Distance Walkers' Association which has a handy index of every long-distance path in Britain – from 2km to 4,498km.

⌀ **lightmyfire.com** Highly recommended sporks and ingredient carriers from Swedish brand Light My Fire.

⌀ **metoffice.gov.uk** Good for tide tables and weather predictions.

⌀ **mountainbothies.org.uk** Become a member of the Mountain Bothies Association (MBA) to help maintain the 100+ mountain huts found here in Britain, and scout one out close to your next adventure.

⊘ **mwis.org.uk** Invaluable resource for mountain-specific weather in Britain.

⊘ **nationalparks.gov.uk** A guide to all the UK's national parks.

⊘ **nature.scot/camping-scotland** A great downloadable guide on camping responsibly in Scotland (which is easily applicable elsewhere, too).

⊘ **rspb.org.uk** The Royal Society for Protection of Birds has a great wildlife guide to help identify birds you may see or hear when in the wilds.

⊘ **stasherbag.com** A great alternative to plastic bags for storing and transporting food once opened.

⊘ **tidetimes.co.uk** Tidal charts for more than 700 locations around the UK.

⊘ **visitengland.com** Official site for Visit England.

⊘ **visitscotland.com** Official site of Scotland's tourist board.

⊘ **visitwales.com** Official site of Wales's tourist board.

⊘ **wildlifewatch.org.uk/spotting-sheets** Fantastic downloadable wildlife-, flower- and plant-spotting guides from the Wildlife Trusts.

⊘ **wildswim.com** Put together by the Outdoor Swimming Society, this constantly updated map lists great places for a spot of swimming (and cooking if used in conjunction with this book…).

⊘ **woodlandtrust.org.uk** A wonderful charity dedicated to protecting our forests and the wildlife that lives within them; also has a handy tree identifier and downloadable map.

## APP

**OS Maps App** A vital resource to help you find your way and plot your route in the wilds – with full OS mapping for the whole of Britain for a small annual subscription fee.

## BOOKS

Mabey, Richard *Food for Free* (Collins Gem, 2012). A handy-sized book great for a beginner forager.

Mears, Ray and Hillman, Gordon *Wild Food* (Hodder, 2008). A fascinating look at the history of foraging and tips on doing it yourself from the bushcraft master himself.

# LIST
## OF
# RECIPES

# INDEX

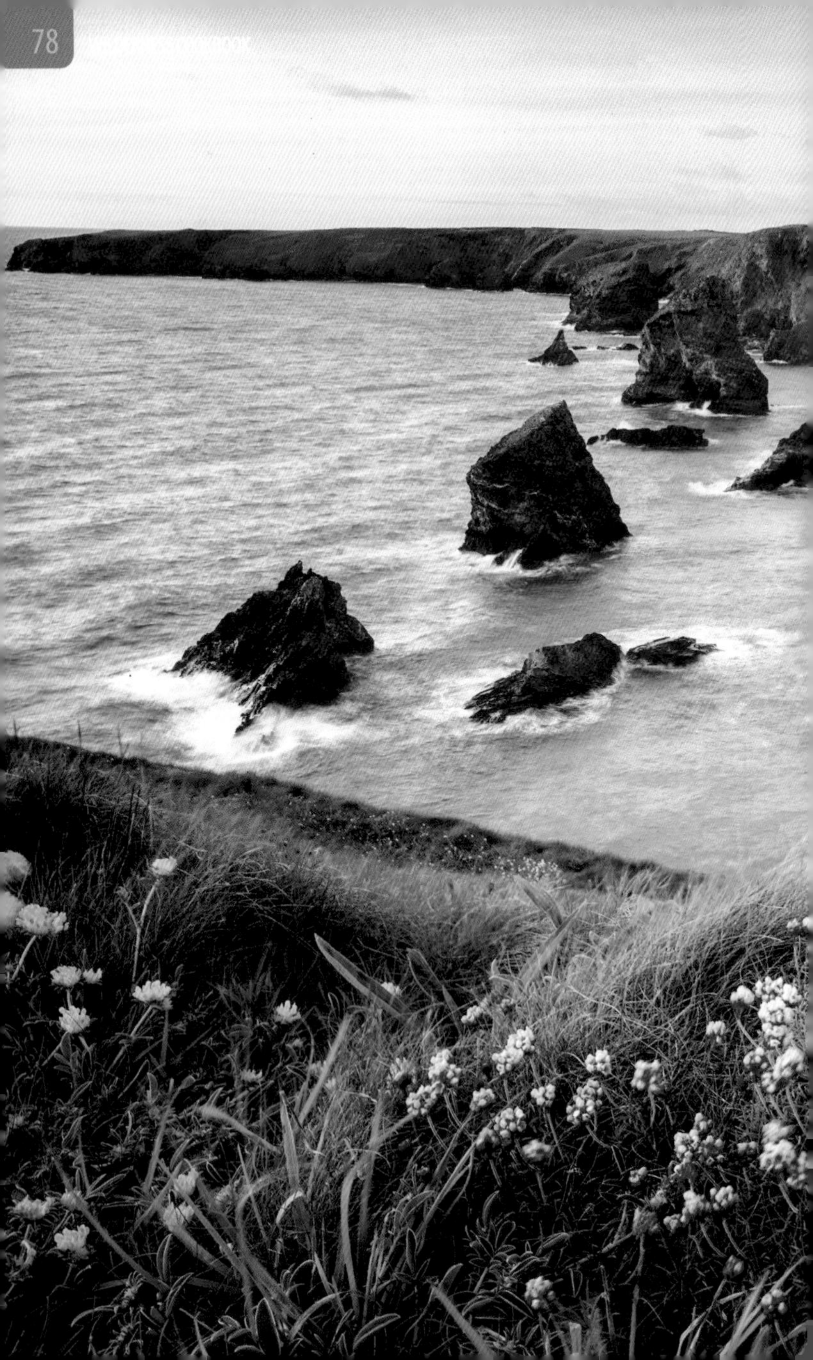